War and Wartime Changes

The Transformation of Arkansas

1940–1945

C. Calvin Smith

The University of Arkansas Press

Fayetteville, 1986

Designer: Joanna V. Hill
Typeface: Linotron Times Roman
Typesetter: G & S Typesetters, Inc.
Printer: Thomson-Shore, Inc.
Binder: John H. Dekker & Sons, Inc.

The paper used in this publication meets the minimum requirements of the American National Standard for Permanence of Paper for Printed Library Materials Z39.48-1984. ∞

LIBRARY OF CONGRESS CATALOGING-IN-PUBLICATION DATA

Smith, Calvin, 1943–
    War and wartime changes.

    Bibliography: p.
    Includes Index.
    1. World War, 1939–45—Arkansas.
2. Arkansas—History. I. Title.
D769.85.A7S54   1986   976.7′052   85-16474
ISBN 0-938626-56-6

To Earline and Calvin Jr., for all the times
that I've said I do not have time, and for
their continued love and support

Contents

Acknowledgments

I wish to express my appreciation to Dr. Timothy P. Donovan, Chairman, Department of History, University of Arkansas, Fayetteville. Without his constructive criticism of the original manuscript, this book would have lacked many of its features. I am also grateful to Dr. Willard B. Gatewood, Jr., for his invaluable aid in helping me locate and interpret primary source materials. I am especially indebted to my wife, Earline, for helping me with matters of style and form. B. Sue Hogue and Kimberly Cummings typed the manuscript and caught many errors that otherwise might have gone unnoticed. The remaining errors and omissions are solely my responsibility.

A list of acknowledgments would not be complete without giving recognition to Mr. Sam Sizer, who was in charge of Special Collections, Mullins Library, University of Arkansas at Fayetteville, where much of the research for this book was done. His assistance in locating and directing me to important documents and manuscript collections was invaluable. I would also like to thank the staff of the Dean B. Ellis Library, Arkansas State University, the Arkansas History Commission, and the National Archives for their valuable assistance and patience.

C. CALVIN SMITH

Preface

There is a significant gap in scholarly works on the recent history of Arkansas. For the period between the depression of the 1930s and the Little Rock desegregation crisis of the 1950s, the literature is almost nonexistent. The *Arkansas Historical Quarterly* has published some articles on the period, but no comprehensive study has been made and published. This book is designed to remedy, at least partially, that vacuum. The focus is on the period between 1940 and 1945, the turbulent years of the Second World War. The war years brought rapid political and socioeconomic changes to Arkansas, and this study analyzes the impact of those changes on the state and the reaction of Arkansans to them. If, as some historians have maintained, World War I propelled the United States into the twentieth century, then World War II had a similar effect upon rural agricultural Arkansas, which lagged behind the rest of the nation in socioeconomic development.

In 1939, when World War II erupted in Europe, the vast majority of Arkansans were still struggling against the misery of ten years of severe depression. They expressed little concern about the turn of events in Europe. To them the immediate challenge was how to escape their economic misfortune. The war, they felt, was a European affair and none of their business. Most believed that it would be a mistake for the United States to become involved as it had during World War I. But, as the European democracies fell one by one to the German war machine, Arkansans, along with the rest of the nation, began to fear for their own safety, and when the federal government launched a massive national defense program in 1940, they were most supportive. The program brought defense industries to Arkansas, ended the problems of unemployment and depression, diversified the state's agricultural-dependent economy, and initiated a new era of prosperity.

On December 7, 1941, Japan launched a surprise attack on the United States naval base at Pearl Harbor, Hawaii, and the national defense industries suddenly became war industries. The war, thanks to its demand for soldiers and workers in war industries, generated rapid economic growth in Arkansas and created a severe shortage of agricultural and domestic workers. One of the purposes of this study is to investigate the impact of those wartime changes in the state's agricultural economy, its agricultural-business interests, and the labor force.

The war also forced the federal government to move toward making the nation more democratic in its economic, social, and political practices at home. Many of these federal changes forced the states to make alterations in their own socioeconomic and political institutions. How did Arkansans react to progressive changes forced upon them by the government and federal courts? Were they readily accepted as wartime necessities, accepted as long overdue, or were they rejected by the state's political leaders and the majority of its citizens? Were any of the changes permanent?

To answer the above questions I have carefully studied the public actions and reactions of Arkansas' business and political leaders and the attitudes and opinions of Arkansans who expressed their views in letters to the editors of local or state newspapers. Editorials in the state's print media have also been used to help determine what Arkansans were thinking during World War II. Unfortunately, few of Arkansas' political leaders maintained constituent files. But those records that are available have been studied extensively and are frequently quoted. Also of great importance were the personal interviews with participants in and eyewitnesses to the history-making events of the Second World War. Those interviews were especially valuable because they were not only informative, but also because they allowed me to look into the eyes of those with whom I talked and sense their joys and sorrows, giving me a better understanding of them and their times.

War and Wartime Changes

1

Drifting Toward War

When the second great war of the twentieth century began in 1939, few Arkansans felt a need to be concerned. The fact that war was raging in Europe did not escape the attention of the rank and file; it was just that they believed it was another European war which would soon be over. They also believed that World War I had been a European war and that American involvement had been a mistake. They did not want history to repeat itself. The majority of the state's population supported the position of Congressman John L. McClellan concerning the first in a series of neutrality laws that Congress passed in 1935. Discussing the law before a cheering crowd at a Labor Day rally in his home district, McClellan said, "The American people are convinced that they cannot reform the world and make it safe for democracy." [1] The people saw the prospects of United States involvement in another European war as appalling. "War to me is hell," commented one Arkansan, "and hell is the last place I choose to fight." [2] Perhaps he felt that the effects of lingering depression in his state were "hell" enough.

Although the outbreak of war in Europe caused an increase in European purchases of American industrial and agricultural supplies, the effects were minimally felt in depression-riddled Arkansas. Times were still very hard. In late 1939, the state, with a population of almost two million, had 90,000 unemployed persons and 67,000 employed on only a part-time basis. An additional 30,000 were on the direct relief rolls of the federal government. [3] These figures refer only to those actually employed or who were actively seeking employment; they do not include the thousands who, due to frustration over the lack of success in finding jobs, had ceased to look for them. To these people the war in faraway Europe meant very little.

When the first signs of war in Europe appeared in the mid-1930s, isolationist sentiments in Arkansas and the nation became more pronounced. And when war in Europe seemed to be inevitable, America expressed its determination not to become involved through the passage of a series of neutrality laws between 1934 and 1937. These laws were opposed by President Franklin D. Roosevelt, but he realized that they expressed the sentiments of the nation at large. He did not openly challenge them, but he did look for ways to soften their impact. With characteristic caution, Roosevelt began in 1937 to try to awaken the country to the dangers of inaction. Following the acceleration of the Japanese invasion of China, the president made his "Quarantine Speech" in Chicago on October 5, 1937, an address calling for the quarantining of aggressor nations by the international community. It was not well received by the public. But when Poland and Finland fell to the rampaging forces of Germany and Russia during the nightmarish winter of 1939–1940, a few people in Arkansas and the nation joined with the president in trying to free the country from its isolationist trance. "Neutrality," declared an editorial in the *Fayetteville Daily Democrat,* "is no guarantee of peace as witnessed by Finland, the most completely neutral nation to be found." The editorial called upon the United States to go to the aid of Finland "and do it now." Dr. John J. Reynolds, president of Hendrix College at Conway, Arkansas, requested the United States to aid Finland because it had a moral obligation to do so. "If America had not held itself aloof from peace efforts and the responsibilities commensurate with her powers and duties [after WW I]," he said, "there would be no war and Hitler would not exist as a political power." The *Arkansas Gazette* also called for United States aid to the European democracies.[4]

These demands for American intervention into the war on behalf of the European democracies evoked as much criticism as sympathy for those besieged nations. One Arkansan even accused the state's interventionist papers of ignoring the sentiments of the majority of the state's population and of using the war as a device to increase sales. "Our official class," wrote Dr. F. W. Buercklin of Portia to the editor of the *Arkansas Gazette,* "seems more susceptible to war propaganda than the people themselves. This is probably due to the people's belated efforts for peace being baffled or scuttled in the interests of our news agencies, whose financial interests are promoted more through the excitement of war than peace."[5] Another staunch noninterventionist, H. F. Rowland of Harrison, accused the papers and others of forgetting that World War I had failed to make the world safe for democracy. "I think," he said, "1917 and 1918 should be a lesson to us to let Europe settle her troubles without our sticking our necks out."[6] Another critic of interventionism accused the press of practicing jingoism.[7] Still another urged pro-interventionists to stop promoting war and to use their talents "to help rid our state and nation of such undemocratic measures as the poll tax and to let Europe solve her own problems this time." [8]

Although the majority of Arkansans were willing to let the European nations fight their own war without American assistance, they shared the growing belief of their countrymen that the United States could not successfully defend itself if attacked by a powerful foreign enemy. Most shared the sentiments of the editor of the *Marked Tree Tribune* when he declared that "America wants to be left alone, but here she lies sprawled like a fat pig in the sunshine, soft and rich picking for today's bandit armies." [9] To protect itself from those "bandit armies" and to make sure that the United States did not accidentally become involved in the European war, Congress passed the Neutrality Act of 1939. The new legislation prohibited American ships from sailing to belligerent ports in Europe. The law did, however, allow belligerents to purchase goods in the United States on a "cash and carry" basis. President Roosevelt signed the bill into law on November 4, 1939. Like the editor of the *Marked Tree Tribune*, Roosevelt realized that the nation was in no position to fight a war at home or abroad. The Neutrality Act of 1939 gave him time to prepare the nation's defensive capabilities while limiting the possibilities of American involvement in Europe.

Preparedness for defense had actually begun in August 1939 when Roosevelt quietly established the War Resources Board (WRB) as a civilian advisory commission to the Army–Navy Munitions Board. The purpose of the WRB was to develop a comprehensive plan of industrial mobilization for war. By 1940 the president was ready to launch a national defense program; all that was needed was the right moment to ensure public support. After the fall of France and the Scandinavian countries to the Germans in the spring of 1940, Roosevelt felt that the moment had arrived that would guarantee public support. In May 1940, he called Congress into special session and requested that it approve a defense program calling for the construction of a two-ocean navy and the building of 50,000 airplanes annually. The president's message to Congress was received with thundering applause, and it was equally popular in Arkansas. Only a few die-hard noninterventionists in the state refused to support the program.

One of the most vocal critics of the national defense program in Arkansas was Paul Ladd, state chairman of the local "Keep America Out of War" Committee. He charged that the defense program was designed to promote war hysteria in the nation with the goal being American involvement in the European war. Ladd, however, was not the state's only critic of the defense program. Echoing the 1934 report of the Nye Committee, which charged that American bankers and munition makers had greedily led the nation into World War I, George H. Couch of Bryant charged that the program was designed "to protect American loans to and capitalist investments in England and France." [10] But such voices of disapproval were few as the great majority of the state's people supported the program because they actually had come to fear a German invasion of American soil by the summer of 1940.

The invasion scare was revealed at Cabot when an Arkansas businessman decided to use airplanes and parachutes to advertise the opening of a new business. The planes descended over the small town one evening just after sunset and released thousands of miniature parachutes with attached business advertisements. To those on the ground, peering through the setting sun, the parachutes appeared to be "chute troops" falling from high-flying German planes, and a little imagination did the rest. People stricken with fear fled into their homes, into nearby woods, into storm cellars; they scrambled for any cover available. It took hours before the local residents realized that the falling parachutes were part of a promotion gimmick. [11] The incident clearly demonstrated how conscious Arkansans had become of the war in Europe and what they believed to be their own vulnerability.

If the United States were invaded, many Arkansans believed it would come as the result of fifth column activity. They were aware of the fate of Norway which had succumbed to the Nazis in 1940. The Norwegians, according to widely circulated newspaper accounts, had been betrayed from within by fifth columnists under the leadership of Vidkun Quisling, and Arkansans were determined that history would not repeat itself in America, especially in Arkansas. Governor Carl E. Bailey ordered the state police to investigate possible fifth column activity in Arkansas. He also urged the Reserve Officers Association, the Arkansas National Guard, the American Legion, and "all other good citizens" to report instances of subversive activity. [12] Bailey issued his order-request in May 1940, and in June, state Attorney General Jack Holt reported that his office was receiving signed letters containing "names and hard statements of fact," disclosing alleged fifth column activities. [13] The governor's appeal for help in identifying potential subversives was superfluous because by the summer of 1940 anyone in Arkansas who did not preach God, Flag, and Country, and not necessarily in that order, was automatically suspected of being disloyal and pro-German.

The case of Frank Lewis serves as a typical example of the aggressive and pervasive anti-German sentiment. Lewis was a fifty-one-year-old German immigrant who lived and worked as a blacksmith in Danville. Following the fall of France to the Nazis, verbal abuse against everything German could be heard in the city. When Lewis attempted to separate the German government from the German people and defend the latter, he was attacked by Odel Lewis (no relation), a local pistol-packing druggist and veteran of World War I who used his revolver to crush the skull of the defender of the German people. To the druggist, all Germans and German sympathizers were Nazis. Frank Lewis died from the assault, but the Yell County Grand Jury refused to indict Odel Lewis for either first- or second-degree murder.

Another, far less serious incident that reflected the depths of anti-German sentiment in Arkansas was the case of Charlotte Anne Von Mikusch-Buchberg. Mrs. Mikusch-Buchberg was granted a divorce from her husband Johannes after she charged that he was a German by birth and a Nazi sympathizer who had lived in the United States for five years without attempting to apply for American citizenship. She also charged that her husband treated her cruelly because she refused to support the Nazis.[14] Apparently Arkansas juries felt that Frank Lewis got what he deserved and that Mrs. Mikusch had undisputable grounds for divorce. Despite the aggressive anti-German feelings among the state's rank and file, there was no overpowering desire on the part of most Arkansans to become militarily involved in what they still viewed as Europe's war.

After the fall of France to the Nazis, President Roosevelt felt that England would soon crumble under the smashing blows of the German war machine if she did not get aid from the United States. The president's views were shared by some prominent Arkansans. An editorial in the *Arkansas Gazette* called for American intervention into the European war as early as June 1940. After vividly describing the horrors and destruction of the American Civil War, which was fought primarily on southern soil and was something with which white Arkansans could identify, the editorial asked, "Could not America best defend itself by fighting on foreign soil rather than wait until the destruction comes home?"[15] And J. William Fulbright, who was then the president of the University of Arkansas, warned that if America failed "to give immediate assistance to England by sending our naval and military planes, and the British Empire is destroyed . . . the only hope for this nation is to consolidate the Western Hemisphere under our control." The attempts of the *Gazette* and Fulbright to convince Arkansans that it was better, cheaper, and less destructive to fight abroad rather than at home generated little support. The majority of Arkansans shared the views of the nation: preparedness for defense, not offense.[16] A strong national defense also called for an increase in the manpower of the armed forces. To achieve that end, Congress in 1940, after heated debate, passed the Burke-Wadsworth Bill (Selective Service Act of

1940), authorizing a one-year peacetime military draft. Although the draft law was adamantly opposed by isolationists, there was little opposition to it in Arkansas. In fact, both Arkansas senators and the state's entire congressional delegation voted for the measure.[17]

While Congress debated the Selective Service Act, the Nazis increased their pressure on Great Britain. The British, weakening under the Nazi air attack, believed that the Germans were planning a cross-channel invasion. To counter such an attack the British desperately needed to strengthen their naval forces and appealed to President Roosevelt for help. America's naval arsenal had a surplus of World War I vintage destroyers, but the president could not make these available to the British due to a provision of the neutrality laws that prohibited the transfer of United States naval property to another nation without the consent of the army and navy chiefs of staff. Roosevelt desperately wanted to transfer the surplus ships to the British but his hands were tied, although not for long. Pressed by the president, Attorney General Robert Jackson found a "clear path" through the maze of neutrality laws that allowed Roosevelt to do as he wished. Jackson discovered that the president could transfer the ships to the British, without the approval of the chiefs of staff, and not be in violation of the neutrality laws because the ships had not been specifically constructed for a foreign power.[18] Armed with Jackson's ruling, and without the approval of Congress, Roosevelt in September 1940 transferred fifty World War I destroyers to the British in exchange for ninety-nine-year leases on British naval and air bases that stretched along the Atlantic from Newfoundland to British Guiana.

The Destroyers-for-Bases Deal generated a storm of criticism because it was clearly a major step away from neutrality and toward belligerency. In fact, after the arrangements were completed, United States neutrality was hardly more than a technicality.[19] But there was little protest from Arkansans. Apparently they agreed with the opinion of the editor of the *Northwest Arkansas Times,* who commented, when rumors of the deal first surfaced, that "the United States' first line of defense on the Atlantic coast is England's continued control of the seas, and as long as conquerors face this barrier, our shoreline from Canada to Florida is comparatively safe." As far as the people of Arkansas were concerned, they agreed with the president when he argued that the agreement would not only strengthen America's defenses but was also a good business deal. The state's senators and representatives also felt that way because all voted for the transfer.[20] But the next move of the administration to aid the British separated the state's rank and file from their political spokesmen and generated heated debate.

On January 6, 1941, President Roosevelt informed Congress and the nation, through his State of the Union message, of his plans to lend or lease vital war supplies to the British. Roosevelt could have requested Congress to modify the nation's neutrality laws so that England could have received more credits in the United States, but he chose not to in order to avoid the problem of war debt collection that had severely strained the nation's relations with its World War I allies. The move also bypassed the Johnson Act of 1934 which forbade loans to any nation which had defaulted on its war debts. The Lend-Lease Bill was formally introduced into Congress on January 11, 1941, and touched off two months of acrimonious debate in Congress and the nation before gaining final approval. Again, Arkansas' business and political leaders supported the president's proposal just as they had supported the Destroyers-for-Bases Deal. An editorial in the *Southwest American* (Fort Smith) urged the public to support Lend-Lease because "a world without Britain is a world infinitely less safe, less pleasant, and less liveable." Therefore, the United States should "aid Britain come Hell or High Water." The *Benton County Democrat* also editorially urged support for the president's proposal because it believed the Nazis had already made plans to conquer the United States by way of South America. The editorial quoted a statement of pro-German sentiment allegedly made by a prominent resident of Rio de Janeiro who said: "We needn't worry about the air raids and bombings here. When Hitler wants Brazil, he can take it by telephone." [21] But it was an Arkansas Fifth District congressman, Clyde T. Ellis, who best summed up the case for Lend-Lease. "Britain," he told one of his constituents, "cannot stop him [Hitler] alone, only the United States stands between him and total submission." [22] The pro-British, pro-Lend-Lease views expressed by the state's newspapers and politicians, however, were apparently not shared by all of the state's citizens.

Many Arkansans agreed with the sentiments of Montana's isolationist Senator Burton K. Wheeler who declared that the results of Lend-Lease "will be to plow under every fourth American boy." [23] "Congress," said one critic of Lend-Lease, "has made the Declaration of Independence a scrap of paper and the Constitution a thing of mockery." Congressman Ellis was one of the more outspoken supporters of Lend-Lease in Arkansas and one of his constituents told him, "Don't get yourself too far out on a limb because a great majority of the inarticulate are bitterly opposed to Lend-Lease." And this, he warned Ellis, "is the great silent vote which fools many politicians." Perhaps it was Laurence Witherspoon, a Little Rock contractor, who best summarized these views. Witherspoon wrote Congressman Ellis in February 1941 requesting that he vote against Lend-Lease because "foreign misunderstandings, for the most part, are of old vintage, too bitter and too deep rooted to be affected by our own likes and dislikes." He also told the congressman that he was opposed to the "British Aid Bill and to similar legislation which will immediately or eventually involve us in the present war." [24]

Proponents of Lend-Lease defended it on the grounds that democracy had to be saved in England if it was to be preserved at home. But that argument was unconvincing to a large number of Arkansans. One critic, voicing the America-first sentiments that dominated the thinking of many people, suggested that the United States forget about Lend-Lease and use American resources for self-defense. "Once successfully prepared for self-defense," he argued, "no bully would dare attack . . . and we would have our own self-respect and could tell the rest of the world to go to hell and stay put." He also called Lend-Lease a cowardly act and said that the nation should be ashamed to "even suggest that we furnish arms for another to fight our battles." [25] Most of the critics of Lend-Lease, however, focused their attention on the argument that it was necessary for the preservation of democracy in England and the United States. "Democracy, what does it mean?" asked one skeptical critic. "Does it mean that we sanction the kind of democracy that England practices in India and Ireland, that one which keeps 400,000,000 people in subjection and slavery, not one of whom apparently believes sufficiently in that form of democracy to offer to help England beat off the other bad form of government?" [26] If that was what Lend-Lease was designed to preserve, the critic clearly indicated that he wanted no part of it. As for the commitment of the United States to democracy, another suspicious Arkansan asked:

> As long as we have more crime than any nation; so much ignorance which can be exploited by leaders; scheming partisan politics; and so many conflicting reports that one can hardly learn the truth, should we boast about our democracy? [27]

Others charged that American and British determination to defeat the Germans grew not from a desire to preserve democracy but from envy of Hitler on the part of their leaders. [28]

Between 1939 and 1941, a good many Arkansans viewed the war as a European affair in which the United States should not become involved. They supported the national defense program, which officially began in the spring of 1940, and the Destroyers-for-Bases Deal in the fall of 1940, because they viewed both as barriers against direct involvement. Like many others in the nation, some believed that if the United States were militarily strong it could force the aggressive dictatorial powers of Europe to limit their activities to that part of the world. Even after the German attack on the American destroyer *Greer* in September and the sinking of the *U.S.S. Kearney* in October 1941, both of which were escorting Lend-Lease materials to England, and after President Roosevelt's declaration that "the shooting has started," most hoped that war could still be avoided. They preferred to believe one of their congressmen who told them in his November 1941 newsletter that "nature has so separated us geographically and Hitler has such a thorough monopoly on Europe that we likely won't cross each other's paths often in the near future." [29] The future, however, was much closer than most imagined, and the incident that would bring the nation into a military confrontation with the Axis powers took place not in Europe or America but in the Far East.

Pearl Harbor: The War Comes Home

While the Roosevelt administration desperately sought ways to keep England from collapsing under the weight of the Nazi juggernaut after 1940, the United States' relations with Japan were rapidly deteriorating. They had taken a turn for the worse in the early 1930s when Japan initiated an aggressive expansion program in Asia that accelerated after the Japanese invasion of China in 1937. President Roosevelt's famous "Quarantine Speech" of October 5, 1937, was directed chiefly at the Japanese. The United States supported China in the Japanese-Chinese conflict, but most of the materials that fueled the Japanese war machine came from America. The situation presented the president with a serious dilemma. Roosevelt was prevented from taking strong actions to counter Japanese activities in China by the 1911 commercial treaty with Japan that did not expire until 1940. It was through this treaty that Japan received most of its war materials. Because of these commitments, the United States in 1938 supplied Japan with 90 percent of its scrap metal and 66 percent of its oil as well as other supplies that could be converted to military use. The president could have invoked the Neutrality Act of 1937, which prohibited the shipment of American military supplies to any belligerent nation, but he did not do so because it would have done more harm to China than to Japan. Therefore, Roosevelt decided to augment China's ability to resist Japanese aggression through the increased shipment of licensed munitions sales. Between July and November 1937, the value of munitions sent to China was $86 million; to Japan, $1.5 million. [30] But the increase in the flow of military supplies to China did little to deter Japanese activity, because Japan had a stockpile of war materials and a much larger industrial capacity than China. The 1911 commercial treaty with Japan, therefore, continued to be a source of

embarrassment for the president because it fueled a war machine that he adamantly opposed.

On July 26, 1939, with widespread public support, the administration gave
Japan the required six-months notice for the termination of the treaty. Sales to
Japan, however, were not immediately cut off in January 1940. The importance of non-renewal weighed heavily on the minds of Japanese militarists.
They realized that the loss of American imports, especially oil and scrap
metal, would severely curtail their expansion program if new supplies were
not found quickly. Faced with such a threat and determined not to withdraw
from China, as the United States demanded, Japan moved to acquire new
sources of raw materials as soon as it could. The success of the Nazi war machine against the Low Countries and France in the spring and summer of 1940
provided Japan with the opportunity.

The fall of the French and Dutch to the Germans left their possessions in
the Far East unprotected and easy prey for Japan. England, nearly fatally weakened, was in no position to resist Japanese advances. With the belief that the
United States would not stand idly by while she completed her aggression
against China and other areas in East Asia, Japanese militarists moved to protect themselves by establishing ties with the Fascist powers of Europe. In September 1940, Japan signed the Tripartite Pact with Germany and Italy. Japan
recognized German and Italian leadership in Europe in return for recognition
of Japanese dominance in Asia. This alliance was obviously aimed at the
United States because it specifically excluded Russia and pledged the signato-
ries to come to the defense of any member attacked by a power that was not
currently involved in the European war or the Sino-Japanese conflict. To neu-
tralize their old enemy Russia, Japan signed a neutrality pact with the Soviets
in April 1941, which called for neutrality if either member was attacked by
another power or powers. This pact worked to the advantage of Russia when
Germany attacked in June 1941, but it also left Japan free to pursue its own
plans for Asia.[31]

The Tripartite Pact and the Japanese neutrality agreement with the Soviets
placed the United States and Japan on a collision course in East Asia. Encouraged by its Axis partnership, Japan pressured Vichy France to allow virtual
Japanese domination of Indo-China, forced the British to close the Burma
Road, one of the last lifelines to beleaguered China, and applied pressure
upon the Dutch government-in-exile for oil and rubber concessions in the
Netherlands East Indies. President Roosevelt, furious over Japan's actions, reacted by placing an embargo on the shipment of aviation fuel, scrap metals,
and all other vital materials to Japan. He also sent a tough diplomatic message

to the Japanese, warning them that "threats to American sources of essential primary commodities in Southeast Asia—all rubber and tin—would not be tolerated." [32] These actions brought American-Japanese relations to an impasse, while each waited for the other to make the next move.

Meanwhile, extensive press coverage of the Far Eastern situation contributed significantly to the growth of a hostile public attitude toward the Japanese by late 1940. In Arkansas it was reflected in a *Northwest Arkansas Times* editorial on December 2, 1940, which addressed the question of statehood for Hawaii. The editorial urged the proponents of Hawaiian statehood to forget the idea because "the Islands have too many Japanese," and further implied that the Japanese could not be trusted. Those views were stated by Arkansas congressman Clyde T. Ellis in a speech on the floor of the House of Representatives in May 1941. Reacting to an invitation from Japan's prime minister, Prince Fumimaro Konoye, to President Roosevelt to come to Japan and discuss a settlement of the differences between the two nations, Ellis urged the president to decline the invitation because it "was only a cover to hide Japanese war intentions." The congressman also declared that he believed "there is a fifty-fifty chance we are headed for deadly combat with Hitler [and] in that event Japan is pledged to stab us in the back." [33] Dr. Sam Hilburn, a Methodist missionary who had returned to Arkansas from Japan in 1941, told a Methodist convention in Fayetteville that the president should not go to Japan because "Japan was a low-rating nation that had turned from God and could not be trusted." The *Arkansas Gazette* editorially urged the president to reject the Japanese invitation if it meant compromise on the China issue. "We cannot agree to peace on the basis of Japan's taking China as a prize of conquest. National self-respect," said the editorial, "would forbid it even if there were no material and practical reasons." [34]

Clearly, the crucial issue that plagued Japanese-American relations was Japanese aggression against China. The national and state press often described the Chinese as a noble, peace-loving people and the Japanese as militant aggressors and sex fiends. [35] By the fall of 1941, public opinion in Arkansas and the nation had become aggressively anti-Japanese. Japan, however, was not yet ready to commit itself to war with the United States over China and East Asia. The moderate Konoye government continued to seek a negotiated settlement of differences with the United States while it tried to restrain Japanese militarism at home.

When the Konoye government failed to reach a satisfactory agreement with the United States by late fall, it was replaced by Japanese militarists under the leadership of General Hideki Tojo, whose government decided that if a settlement with the United States could not be reached by the end of November, they would go to war. In the meantime, American intelligence was able to break the Japanese secret diplomatic cipher through a device code named "Magic," which, in late November, revealed that Japan had made the decision for war. No one knew precisely where the Japanese would strike. American military officials anticipated an attack, possibly a surprise one, on Malaya, Thailand, the Dutch East Indies, or the Philippines, or perhaps against all of them. On December 7, 1941, the Japanese hit the one area no one expected—the American naval base at Pearl Harbor. Only after the attack did Japan announce that it had declared war on the United States and England. On December 8, 1941, the United States declared war on Japan. A few days later Germany and Italy also declared war on the United States. America, thanks to the Japanese, was now involved in another world war. But in Arkansas and the nation the immediate focus of attention was on Japan, not the Axis powers of Europe. The Japanese, according to an *Arkansas Gazette* editorial, had committed a form of national hara-kiri. The attack on Pearl Harbor, declared the editorial, "was one of the most insane acts in all the history of nations, but vengeance will be deliberate and ordered—and unsparing and to the death, no matter what the cost and sacrifice." [36]

After Pearl Harbor there was an almost unanimous cry for retaliation. In Arkansas, veterans of World War I expressed a desire to be young again so they could subdue the "Yellow Peril." The state's youth also responded with patriotic fervor. Records were set at military recruiting offices throughout the state. The marines reported that they were "troubled with too many enthusiastic youths of sixteen that we cannot take." But young men continued to try to enlist in any branch of the service that would take them. The entire Lepanto (Arkansas) High School football team volunteered for naval duty. When one of them was rejected because he was unable to pass the physical exam, he drank carbolic acid. "I was afraid folks would think I was yellow because I didn't get in the service," he told hospital attendants, "and I just couldn't take that." [37] Fortunately, few went to the extremes of the Lepanto youth.

Adults who were unable to join the armed forces due to age, physical disability, or for other reasons often took to print to express their hatred of the Japanese and their support of the war effort. Hundreds of anti-Japanese poems and letters were written by Arkansans and sent to local papers for publication. A typical example was one written by a Little Rock resident which read:

> Taint no use to grumble,
> Taint no use to cry

After you hear the rumble
Of the Japs goin' by.

Just grab a gun
If not, a wrench.
Put 'em on the run,
They raised the stench!

O'er in the Pacific wide,
At Pearl Harbor, you know,
Dern their yellow hides,
Let's get 'em on the go.

On to Tokio! Yes, Tokio!
Chase 'em left and right
Let the little bastards know
They still have MacArthur to fight.[38]

Some of the poems and letters reflected the widespread belief that the war would be a short one due to American racial and military superiority. A poem written by a resident of Kensett, allegedly at the behest of neighbors, and sent to the *Arkansas Gazette*, requested publication if the editors thought it worthy of space. They did. The poem was titled "Twine for the Japs" and read:

Write a poem about the Japs
What a request of me!
For with nothing for a subject
'Tis hard to write, you see.

When I write of something yellow,
'Twill be an ode to cheese,
But I'll not waste my talents on
A yellow Nipponese!

I could write about a horse thief
A gangster or hobo,
But I can't pen my thoughts about
The imps from Tokio!

I could write about a bed bug,
A maggot or a louse,
A buzzard, a skunk, a viper,
A mosquito or a mouse.

I write of everything,
From elephants to fleas,
But I can't think quite low enough
To reach the Japanese!

When God, the loathsome reptiles made
He gathered up the scraps
And made a bunch of scalawags
And Adam named them Japs.

One day they jumped on Uncle Sam
So they'll be needing twine
For we will break and tie in knots
The string they call their spine![39]

Evidently, most Arkansans viewed the war in Europe as a war between nations, but they looked upon the American battle against Japan as a war between races. The fact that the war in the Far East was underlined with heavy
racial overtones was not lost upon Arkansas' black population.

During the first few months of the war some black Arkansans, reacting to a
history of oppression and racial discrimination, supported Japan. They mistakenly looked upon the Japanese as one of the darker races of the world who
were fighting to free themselves from colonialism and the enforced theory of
white supremacy. Such thoughts, however, did not reflect the views of the majority of blacks. To those who sympathized with the Japanese, the editor of the
State Press, Arkansas' only black newspaper, told them that such ideas were
folly. "Japan is fighting for Hitler and not the darker races and Hitler is fighting for [racial] supremacy." He also told them that "no victory other than a
victory for America will benefit blacks."[40]

The overwhelming majority of black Arkansans, in spite of past injustices,
supported the war effort. A resolution adopted by the black congregation of
Little Rock's First Baptist Church urged blacks to support the war so that they
could receive better treatment in the postwar period. Some even believed that
blacks would suffer—more than usual—if they did not support the war. Dr.
J. B. Watson, president of Arkansas Mechanical and Normal College at Pine
Bluff, the only state-supported institution of higher education for blacks, told
the 1942 graduating class that "this is our war" and that "it would be a tragedy for us Negroes if this war should be won without our having a definite part
in the fight."[41] From Watson's viewpoint, if blacks did not support the war
effort they would be placing another weapon in the hands of their oppressors
to use against them. Even without the encouragement of black leaders, how-

ever, most blacks were more than willing to do their part to support the war due to simple patriotism. Perhaps the sentiments of the majority of black Arkansans were best expressed by a disabled seventy-nine-year-old sharecropper from eastern Arkansas who used part of his monthly relief check to purchase war savings bonds. "I have only one eye and have not worked in four years," he explained, "but I am willing to do all I can to help whip them damn Japs." [42] Black leaders, however, still remembered the discrimination and mob violence that greeted black soldiers and civilians following their participation in the First World War and "this time," declared the editor of the *State Press,* "the black man expects no repetition." [43]

During World War II the majority of black Arkansans lived on the farms and plantations of eastern Arkansas, an area known throughout the state and nation for its oppressive racial policies. It was there that blacks made the greatest effort to support the war. In Forrest City (St. Francis County), blacks purchased $47,000 in war bonds in a single rally. In Marked Tree (Poinsett County), black leaders brought in nationally known columnist Roscoe C. Simmons of the Chicago *Defender* to help promote the sale of war bonds and stamps. The *Defender* was one of the nation's leading black newspapers, well known in Arkansas and throughout the South for its criticism of southern racial practices. Before Simmons arrived in Marked Tree, the local white paper felt it necessary to let the white community know that he was a southerner by birth, understood southern "traditions," and was not coming to town to cause "trouble." As a result of Simmons' appearance, local black sharecroppers, domestics, and others purchased $3,000 in war bonds and stamps in one night. [44] In short, black Arkansans were no different from their white neighbors when it came to supporting the war effort. From their point of view, it was not only white America that had been attacked by Japan; all Americans had been attacked.

In the eight months preceding Pearl Harbor, Arkansans purchased $10 million in defense stamps and bonds, and after the attack purchases skyrocketed. Bankers reported that they were greeted by long lines of customers in front of their establishments waiting to buy stamps and bonds when they arrived to open for the day. To increase sales after Pearl Harbor, patriotic groups developed slick promotional schemes. In late December 1941, in Jonesboro, the local branch of the American Legion formed the "Slap-A-Jap Club." The public was encouraged to join by purchasing one 25¢ defense stamp per week for the duration of the war. [45] The Jonesboro Production Credit Association (PCA) followed with a program to "Slap-The-Jap-With-A-Pig." Pigs, marked with huge "V" for victory on the head and back, were specially fed to produce the greatest possible weight before being auctioned off to the public. All proceeds were used by the PCA to purchase stamps and bonds. The PCA program was so successful that it drew representatives from the Columbia Broadcasting System, *Life* magazine, and other national organizations and publications to Arkansas to cover its auctions.[46]

At times the drive to promote the sale of war stamps and bonds took on a carnival atmosphere, albeit a patriotic one. Capitalizing on the militant anti-Japanese mood, the Batesville Kiwanis Club used a modified version of the old carnival two-balls-for-a-nickel throwing game to raise money for the purchase of stamps and bonds. A life-size picture of General Tojo was painted on a large board in full uniform. A hole in the board served as both the general's mouth and target for the customers. Offering two throws for a nickel and no prize for a direct hit, the stand averaged $15 to $20 each Saturday, the only day it was open.[47] The satisfaction of scoring a direct hit against Japan, if only psychological, was enough for customers.

In addition to the various promotion gimmicks by private groups, Arkansas' public schools and institutions of higher education also participated in the numerous stamp and bond drives. The typical procedure used in the public schools was to assign a quota to each homeroom. The room with the largest total purchase was granted a prize which normally consisted of free tickets to a movie for the group and stars or pins for each participating individual. Colleges and universities held victory dances with the purchase of a 25¢ defense stamp as the minimum price for admission. The schools and colleges were also vigorous participants in the various salvage campaigns during which woods, fields, junkyards, and ditches were scoured for precious scraps of tin, rubber, aluminum, copper, and iron.[48]

The one area in which Arkansans fell somewhat short during the war was in the number of volunteers they contributed to some home front service agencies. Almost everyone was willing to contribute capital through the purchase of stamps and bonds, but not enough people were willing to donate their time. The service agency in Arkansas that most needed volunteers was the Red Cross. During the national defense program thousands of Arkansas women, minus lipstick, rouge, powder, nail polish, and jewelry, and dressed in plain white linen, volunteered for work in Red Cross sewing rooms across the state to make bandages for defense. But after Pearl Harbor, volunteers for the sewing rooms and for Red Cross nurses aides training programs sharply declined. Those who volunteered for the Red Cross programs took a cost-free, seven-week training course. In return for the free training graduates promised to serve a minimum of one hundred and fifty hours per year. Volunteers, how-

ever, were few after the United States declared war on Japan, and approximately only one-third of those who completed the program ever served.[49] Due
to the lack of white women who volunteered for the Red Cross programs, and
white women were the only ones recruited by the agency, the editor of one of
the state's local papers sarcastically said: "Let George do it has been femi-
nized; now it's let Georgia do it." In a later edition the paper again complained
about the lack of volunteers and acidly commented: "For further details con-
sult your conscience."[50]

Recruiters for the Red Cross and other volunteer agencies expected middle-
class housewives and other women with leisure hours to donate their time and
talents. When they failed to produce the desired numbers, little effort was
made to recruit others. Instructors at Shorter College, a small black Methodist
institution in North Little Rock, repeatedly requested the Red Cross to establish classes at the school to train black women in first aid, knitting, and other
war-related projects. When the agency failed to respond to the school's request, black women in the area organized themselves as the MacArthur Knitting Club of Pulaski County and made sweaters for servicemen. In one month
the twenty-five club members knitted twenty-five sweaters and asked the Red
Cross to provide materials for more. Amazingly, the sweaters were made after
the women had spent ten to twelve hours per day on nearby farms and plantations chopping cotton for their daily bread.[51]

Indeed, the great majority of women who voluntarily gave their time and
talents to home front service agencies were those with the least amount of
time to give. The chairperson for Volunteer Services for the Red Cross in
Pulaski County complained that many housewives who could help in the program had accepted the theory of "let the other fellow do it." Most of the work
done in the sewing rooms of the Red Cross in Arkansas was done by girls who
worked a "Victory Shift" in the rapidly growing war industries. They left
their regular jobs at 4:00 p.m., started work in the sewing rooms at 4:30 and
continued until 7:00 p.m. A farm wife in northeast Arkansas who cared for
300 chickens, five hogs, one milk cow, one mule, and who did all the other
required chores so that her husband could work in a war industry also volunteered her services. After reading repeated requests in the local paper for volunteers, she declared that "with the help of God" she would spend a few hours
each week making surgical dressings for the Red Cross. She reportedly hitch-
hiked several miles each day into nearby Jonesboro to keep her pledge. The
important role played by these women was seldom recognized or appreciated
by their peers, but the services they performed were invaluable to the successful execution of Red Cross objectives and the nation's war effort.[52]

The shortage of women in the volunteer services in Arkansas was due to a number of factors, but lack of interest or a patriotic desire to help was not a major one. After Pearl Harbor, the nation's defense industries suddenly became war industries and they, combined with the manpower demands of the armed forces, created a severe shortage of labor on the home front. Consequently, women were called upon to serve as replacements. They filled vacancies in factories, businesses, on the farms, and in other areas where there was a shortage of manpower. In the fall of 1943, the director of the War Manpower Commission for Arkansas reported that over 80,000 women in the state were employed in non-agricultural jobs and that the defense industries were in need of an additional 8,000.[53] With such a demand for women workers for non-agricultural jobs in predominantly rural Arkansas, there was little time or energy left for them to donate to nonprofit service agencies.

2 Mobilizing for Defense and War

Even before World War II began in Europe, President Roosevelt had quietly initiated an assessment of the nation's industrial capacity by creating the War Resources Board (WRB) in August 1939. As a civilian advisory commission to the Army–Navy Munitions Board, its job was to develop a comprehensive plan of industrial mobilization in case of war. When hostilities started in September, the president established the Office of Emergency Management (OEM) which was to coordinate mobilization efforts. Between 1939 and 1940, the WRB and the OEM did little more than collect and file reports with the president. Although the sentiments of the American public favored the European democracies in their struggle against Nazi Germany, public opinion polls showed strong opposition to United States intervention. Therefore, President Roosevelt did not publicly call for general defensive mobilization because he did not want the public to think that he was preparing the nation for intervention. But the fall of France to the Nazis in the spring of 1940 convinced the president that the nation was ready to support a national defense program. His instincts were correct. In May 1940, before a hastily convened joint session of Congress, Roosevelt requested funds to rearm the nation for defense. Congress responded by appropriating $8 billion for defense. Included in the appropriations were funds for the construction of a two-ocean navy, the building of 50,000 airplanes annually, and funds for the construction of new defense industries. Congress also approved a one-year peacetime draft. By the end of 1940, Roosevelt's national defense program was operating successfully, bringing renewed vitality to an economically depressed nation.

The Impact of Military and Industrial Development

To those states that were suffering from the crippling effects of the Great Depression of the 1930s the securing of national defense industries became a major goal. But these industries needed an ample supply of skilled labor, and that presented a serious problem for Arkansas. In 1940, when the defense program began to accelerate, the state had a population of less than 2 million, and four out of every five lived and worked on farms and plantations.[1] Therefore, the movement of defense industries into the state was slow. Arkansas was also handicapped by inexperienced leadership in Washington where many of the contacts with major industries were made. At the beginning of the 1940 congressional session, five of Arkansas' six congressmen were freshmen.[2] New congressmen had little influence in the nation's capital. If those handicaps were not enough, there was still the problem of a negative national image.

Many of the nation's business, industrial, and political leaders—those people who could facilitate the movement of industry into Arkansas—looked upon the state with disdain. Nationally, Arkansans were identified with "watermelons, the unshaven Arkie, the moonshiner, slow trains, malnutrition, mental debility, hookworms, hogs, the big fat lie, shoelessness, illiteracy, windy politicians, and hillbillies with paddlefeet who could not pronounce correctly the name of their state."[3] This view was revealed in Congress when Arkansas congressman Clyde T. Ellis complained about the small number of defense contracts awarded to his state. "Ellis," replied Pennsylvania congressman John R. McDowell, "wants to tear down our factories, throw out of work our working men, close up our mines and our mills, and remove them to the wild hills of the Ozarks where the business and prosperity will rebound to the everlasting glory of the Ozark hillbillies."[4]

Despite the negative reaction that Arkansas businessmen and politicians encountered when they sought defense contracts for the state, they were not deterred and their persistence eventually proved successful. Although the total dollar amount of federal expenditures for defense and war industries spent in Arkansas was small when compared to other states, only 1.16 percent between 1940 and 1945,[5] the economic impact in terms of jobs and income for the state's population was significant (see Table 1).

In addition to the construction projects listed in Table 1, Camp Pike, at Little Rock, which had been an army recruitment and training center during World War I, was renamed Camp Joe T. Robinson and served a similar purpose during World War II. Five air bases were also constructed in the state before 1945, and additional war industries were built in Texarkana, Hope, Camden, El Dorado, and several other cities.[7] By the end of the war Arkansas' agricultural economy had been greatly diversified (see Table 2).

Table 1

Defense Construction Projects in Arkansas, 1940–1945

SITE	DOLLAR AMOUNT	NUMBER OF PERSONS EMPLOYED AT PEAK OF PRODUCTION
Arkansas River (Blue Mountains Dam)	$1,111,897.00	205
Fort Smith (Camp Chaffee)	15,512,786.00	2,005
Jacksonville (Ordnance Plant)	21,297,768.00	13,118
Magnet Cove (Aluminum Plant)	33,000,000.00	1,285
Magnet Cove (Lake Catherine Steam Generating Plant)	(Included in Cost of Magnet Cove Project)	82
Little Rock—Marche (Maumelle Ordnance Plant)	16,750,000.00	3,492
Harrison—Norfork (Dam Construction)	10,778,726.00	1,238
Pine Bluff (Incendiary Munitions Plant)	8,625,000.00	6,380

SOURCE: United States Employment Service Record Group 183, Box 16, Arkansas, National Archives, Washington, D.C.[6]

The movement of wartime industries into Arkansas, with their demands for skilled and unskilled labor, placed a tremendous strain on the state's human and physical resources. Many of the communities where the new industries located did not have the facilities to accommodate management personnel and the influx of job seekers that followed. The most immediate problem was an acute shortage of housing. In April 1940, the United States Census Bureau reported that of the 519,507 habitual dwellings in Arkansas, only 24,791 were vacant. Not many of these were in areas where defense industries located. According to the government, people were not to relocate in defense areas until referred by the United States Employment Service (USES). Few, however, waited for the USES to direct them to jobs. Whenever it was rumored that a defense plant was being constructed, job seekers flocked to the area. In

Table 2

Non-Farm Employment in Arkansas April 1940 and April 1946

INDUSTRY	NUMBER OF EMPLOYERS 1	EMPLOYMENT 2	
		1940	1946
Total, all industries	19,017	272,902	326,200
Mining	289	5,790	7,100
Construction	981	16,557	23,000
Manufacturing	2,174	55,894	69,000
Food	406	6,089	8,400
Apparel	18	1,518	2,500
Lumber Basic Products	1,225	30,015	29,400
Finished Lumber Products	141	4,970	6,700
Paper and Allied Products	8	2,384	2,700
Printing and Publishing	163	2,545	2,800
Chemicals	51	1,665	3,300
Petroleum & Coal Products	10	1,152	1,700
Stone, Clay & Glass Products	50	1,474	2,100
Non-Ferrous Metal Products	9	461	1,500
Other Manufacturing	93	3,621	7,900
Transportation, Communications & Utilities	674	24,085	30,400
Wholesale & Retail Trade	9,124	61,884	76,200
Finance, Insurance & Real Estate	1,055	6,945	7,800
Service (Exc. Domestic & Prof.)	3,293	24,999	31,200
Domestic Service	—	29,118	28,200
Professional Service	1,180	27,297	26,900
Government	—	12,347	18,000
All other	319	7,986	8,400

SOURCE: United States Employment Service, Area Labor Market Survey Reports, Arkansas, Box 15, Folder: Little Rock, Arkansas, National Archives, Washington, D.C.

1940, when the public learned that a munitions plant was being constructed in Pine Bluff, the city was flooded with job-hungry people. The unexpected strain on housing and other facilities was so great that the editor of the *Pine Bluff Commercial* urged people to stay away until referred by USES.[8] His advice was ignored.

Cities with defense industries experienced phenomenal population growth. In Fort Smith, where Camp Chaffee and two aluminum plants were located, the population increased by 5,100 between October 1940 and October 1941.[9] In Hope, the site of the army's Southwestern Proving Grounds, the population grew from 7,475 in 1940 to 15,475 by January 1942. Due to the expansion of Camp Robinson, the establishment of nearby defense industries, and the movement of the families of soldiers and war workers into the city, Little Rock's population increased by 25,000 between June and December of 1940. Families were reduced to living in warehouses, sheds, tents, automobile garages, service stations, and tar-paper structures. The housing situation in Pine Bluff was the worst in the state. In December 1941, the city was classified as a special defense center by the federal government, due to the location of a munitions arsenal, an incendiary bomb plant, and an air base. A former high school principal who had been drafted into the army in 1941 and employed as a research chemist at the arsenal in Pine Bluff reported that he was unable to find housing for himself and his family of four and was forced to live in a barbershop with fourteen other men. Housing of any kind, he said, was not to be found in Pine Bluff.[10]

In addition to the severe shortage of housing, there was also the problem of rapid inflation as property owners increased rental rates in order to profit from the demand for housing. In some areas of the state rates tripled. To limit the spiraling cost of rental property, the federal government ordered a freeze on rents in March of 1942. The freeze, however, was at 1942 levels which were the highest in Arkansas' history. It also penalized those who kept their prewar jobs which paid considerably less than those in the defense industries. These people could not afford to relocate as better housing became available because their income had not kept pace with inflated rental rates. The freeze also caused property owners to delay improvements on rental property because they could not increase rates to cover the cost of repairs. Fortunately for those who came to the defense centers in search of employment, there was no shortage of food. A woman in Pine Bluff was found living in a tar-paper shack serving her family a meal of roast beef, string beans, boiled potatoes, lettuce, carrots, bread, butter, and fresh milk.[11]

Undoubtedly the construction of war industries and military bases in Arkansas brought economic prosperity, but it also caused dislocation and heartaches. Most of the new industries and military establishments were constructed on leased agricultural property close to nearby cities. The owners were asked to relocate. "We hate to leave our land but if Uncle Sam wants it, it's his," was the general attitude, but some people were adamantly opposed to leasing their property to the government.[12] In 1940, the army proposed to lease 39,500 acres of nearby agricultural property for the expansion of Camp

Robinson and for the construction of a training and maneuvering area. Over four hundred residents immediately protested. They believed that their land would be worthless when it was returned to them after the war. Those who had leased their land to the government during World War I argued that the returned land had been unsuitable for farming because of the presence of unexploded shells which made tilling the soil a hazardous undertaking.[13] The owners preferred to sell rather than lease their land.

The government refused to purchase the land needed for expansion of Camp Robinson, thereby forcing the landowners into organized resistance. In November 1940, they organized the Home Owners of Camp Robinson Extension Area Association (HOCREA) and prepared for battle with the government. Spokesmen for the group charged that the government had been misled by reports that the land was largely uninhabited. HOCREA also argued that its members could not afford to move and find new homes because the lease price, which ranged from $15 to $100 per acre, was too low and because no provisions for advanced payments had been made. The government, believing that was the only problem, offered in December of 1940 to pay the landowners the first six months' lease fee in advance and pay the cost of relocation. The fact that its members wanted to sell rather than lease their land was never seriously considered, and HOCREA rejected the government's offer of advanced payments and appealed to the Little Rock Chamber of Commerce for help. But the chamber, with the aid of Arkansas congressman David D. Terry, had lobbied hard for the expansion of Camp Robinson and did not look favorably upon HOCREA's position. In fact, Terry urged the chamber to dismiss HOCREA's appeal because "if every soldier in the camp spends $10 a month, it would mean an increase in income for the city in excess of $4,200,000 a year. That," according to Terry, "was sufficient reason to ignore HOCREA's argument." Consequently, the chamber, aware of the potential bonanza, refused to petition the government to buy rather than lease the property for Camp Robinson's expansion.[14]

Spurned by the federal government and local businessmen, the members of HOCREA took their case to federal court. The court, however, was no more sympathetic than the federal government and the Little Rock Chamber of Commerce. Under a United States District Court condemnation order, members were ordered to lease their property to Camp Robinson and vacate the area by February 1, 1941. The court's ruling resulted in dislocation, disappointment, and bitterness for HOCREA's membership. Their feelings were adequately summed up by Frankie Dean, one of the organization members. "We poor peckerwood Americans are victims of discrimination," he said, "because we're not educated and lodge members." [15] The fate of HOCREA weighed heavily on the minds of others similarly situated. Small farmers and property owners in areas adjacent to industrial plants or military bases lived in a world of uncertainty, not knowing from day to day whether their property would be confiscated for government use or not. Their crops went unattended in the fields, homes remained unrepaired, and neglected livestock roamed freely along roadsides and over unplowed fields. In October 1941, almost a year after HOCREA's members had been ordered to leave their property, Congressman Fadjo Cravens of Fort Smith, where Camp Chaffee was located, urged Secretary of Agriculture Charles R. Wickard to aid the farmers and others who were being uprooted because of military construction. Cravens told Wickard that "unless department [of Agriculture] facilities were lent to aid the people during the transition, a deplorable situation would be aggravated." [16] To assist uprooted farmers, the United States Department of Agriculture and the chambers of commerce in Little Rock and Fort Smith opened up information offices which provided displaced farmers with information on jobs, homes, and farms in other areas. However, this proved to be of little value to the majority of the dispossessed. Few could afford to purchase new homes and farms with the money received from their leased property. Most moved to nearby cities to seek employment in the defense industries where they became just other faces in the crowd. The independence and pride that landownership provided was lost. The story of small farmers who were uprooted by the industrial and military demands of a nation at war is one of the forgotten home front casualties of World War II.

The Urban Migration: State and Local Government Under Stress

The migration of displaced farmers and thousands of unemployed job seekers into defense centers placed a heavy burden on the resources of local government. Due to the shortage of manpower and materials, city officials found it difficult to maintain essential services such as fire and police protection, garbage collection, and street maintenance at normal levels. Especially damaging to city streets in defense centers were large, tax exempt, military vehicles used to transport war materials. [17] City treasuries were soon depleted as local tax revenues, the only source of municipal income, could not keep pace with the costs imposed by a growing population, and voters were reluctant to approve higher taxes. Fire departments were particularly hard pressed to meet the demands placed upon them by the spurt in the construc-

tion of both temporary and permanent housing, and there was a correspond-
ing decline in the quality of other city services.

The war not only denied local government the materials needed to maintain
adequate levels of public services, but it also drained them of their manpower.
The loss of personnel was due both to the requirements of the armed forces
and the inability of local governments to match the higher wages paid by the
war industries. A typical example of the problems faced by local governments
in defense centers throughout Arkansas was that of Fort Smith. Between October 1940 and October 1941, the city's population increased by 5,100, but
during the same period the city suffered a net loss of twenty-one municipal
employees. All of those who resigned were either inducted into the armed
forces or took better paying jobs in local defense industries.

State government faced the same problem. By January 1941, state employment officials reported that they were no longer able to fill state jobs in the
$110 to $150 per month bracket because of competition from the defense industries. These were top-level jobs, and lower-level ones, some paying as
little as $35 per month, simply remained unfilled. The state, like its local gov-
ernments, was unable to increase salaries in order to keep qualified personnel,
because salary levels were fixed by the legislature which only met biannually.
During the 1941 session the legislature had failed to take any action to raise
state salaries, and when it met again in 1943, the situation had become too
critical to be solved by the token increases that were authorized.[18]

The loss of personnel was also felt by private businesses and their customers. In the defense centers, chauffeurs, cab drivers, cooks, housekeepers,
waiters, and waitresses became increasingly rare. Labor was so scarce that
some restaurants put up signs pleading with customers to "Please be Polite to
the Help; We can get Customers." Patrons continuously complained about
poor service. Describing a foray into the field of public food service, one
newspaper reporter wrote, "We have been reached across, reached over, and
reached to at so many restaurant tables that we've acquired an almost bored
attitude toward anything resembling service." When the staffs of the new military bases and war industries first arrived in Arkansas, they were treated roy-
ally by local business leaders, but when local residents began to lose their help
to the newcomers, the welcome mat was withdrawn and the new arrivals became "Damn Yankees." According to the editor of the *Hope Star*, a "Damn
Yankee" in Arkansas was "anyone caught looking over your apartment or in-
terviewing your cook." [19]

Middle and upper middle-class Arkansans who could afford domestics may
have suffered some inconvenience, but their sufferings were minor when com-

pared to the plight of small businessmen who not only lost their employees, but, in many cases, were forced to cease operating completely. Between December 1941 and July 1943, Arkansas' commissioner of revenues, Murray B. McLeod, reported that 6,000 small businesses in the state had been forced to close their doors because of labor shortages. Hardest hit were small community grocery stores, gas stations, and restaurants. The situation became so critical by 1943 that businessmen throughout the state were demanding that the legislature pass laws requiring employees to give notice before quitting and that those who left their old jobs be accepted in new ones only with the approval of their former employees. The legislature refused to pass such a law and the wives and daughters of small businessmen, many of whom had never worked before, were pressed into service in order to keep family businesses open.[20]

While small businessmen struggled to stay in operation, many marginal small farmers gave up the battle and sought employment in the state's war industries. Discouraged by summer droughts and fall floods and lured by shorter working hours and attractive wages, more than 19,700 Arkansas families deserted their farms by 1943, leaving 8,170 farms vacant and 428,528 acres of land untilled.[21] Farm acreage in the state between 1940 and 1945 fell from 18,044,548 acres to 17,761,582.[22] Of the 667,000 persons who comprised the farm population in 1940 only 292,000 were left by the spring of 1944.[23] Many of the state's wealthy planters, however, were able to continue operations by converting to expensive machinery to compensate for the loss of a cheap labor supply.

The manpower demands of the armed forces and the war industries were not the only reasons that caused many large Arkansas agricultural operations to lose part of their labor force. Other major factors were their primitive views toward the cost of labor and their negative attitudes toward their employees. The majority of the state's large agricultural enterprises were located in eastern Arkansas where the labor force was primarily comprised of poor black sharecroppers and day laborers. Influenced by a pervasive racism, the planters were not inclined to pay a competitive wage. As one expressed it, "The only way to keep Negroes on the farm is by paying a starvation wage because when Negroes get a little money they quit work."[24] To make sure that blacks did not leave the plantations for better paying jobs in the war industries, some planters resorted to the practice of peonage.

Peonage in wartime Arkansas was first detected in an extradition hearing for an Arkansas fugitive in Illinois. In May 1943, a Chicago judge refused to release to Arkansas authorities one James Buchanan, a black man arrested on a fugitive warrant from the city of Osceola in eastern Arkansas because he believed that the defendant had been kept in peonage. Buchanan had been jailed in Osceola in December 1941 after surrendering to authorities following a shooting incident. During the extradition hearing, the defendant's lawyers charged that Sheriff Hale Jackson of Osceola had filed no formal charges against Buchanan, but had given him a choice of a long prison sentence or work on his farm. Buchanan testified that he worked for Jackson from December 1941 to February 1943, at which time he fled to Chicago. Sheriff Jackson, who was present at the hearing, denied that Buchanan had been kept in peonage. He even accused Buchanan of being ungrateful. "We were lenient with him around the jail and gave him odd jobs so that he could earn a little money." But when Jackson failed to produce documentation that Buchanan had been charged with a crime in Arkansas, the judge denied the extradition request because "this man was held in virtual peonage in violation of the Constitution which abolished slavery long ago." [25]

Far more serious were the cases of the Clyde Miller and Shelly McKinney families. In March 1944, Albert Sydney Johnson, a planter in the eastern Arkansas county of Cross, was arrested by federal authorities and charged with peonage. He was accused of forcefully holding the Miller and McKinney families on his property for debts they owed him. Testimony during the six-day trial, held in the U.S. District Court of the Mississippi delta town of Helena, revealed that the plantiffs had offered on several occasions to pay their debts to Johnson but that he had refused each offer and demanded labor instead. Testimony also disclosed that Johnson used armed guards to patrol his property to keep tenants from leaving and that he brutally beat tenants if they tried to leave or asked for their wages. The all-white jury found the defendant guilty on two counts of peonage. In announcing sentence, Federal Judge Harry J. Lemley said, "It is the opinion of this Court that the defendant has not only committed the crime of peonage but has done so in an aggravated way. His treatment of the Negroes involved has been so brutal as to require the Court to give him a substantial sentence." Johnson was sentenced to two and one-half years concurrent prison terms on each count. [26] Following the sentence, Sam Rorex, the federal prosecuting attorney in the case, said that Johnson's conviction proved that Arkansans did not condone the practice of peonage. [27] But if Arkansans did not condone the practice, Arkansas law did.

The case against Albert S. Johnson was a federal one, and it was a federal prosecutor, federal jurors, and a federal judge who convicted him. Arkansas law enforcement officials played no part in the case. The conviction of Johnson by a jury of his peers, however, underscored two important facts about agricultural life and race relations in wartime Arkansas. The first was the obvious shortage of cheap agricultural labor and the callous disregard that some planters held for the rights of their black employees. Secondly, it revealed an unprecedented willingness by the agricultural community of eastern Arkansas to try to improve their negative image by convicting one of their own. As for Johnson, his sentence was not as "substantial" as the judge indicated. He served less than a year of his sentence under minimum security. And to the dismay of the planter community, the willingness to convict Johnson did not help to maintain a cheap labor force.[28]

Not only did Arkansans leave the farms during the war in search of employment, they also left the state. The majority of those who left were blacks from eastern Arkansas. Between April 1, 1940, and November 1, 1943, the state lost approximately 10.9 percent of its population. Only five of the state's seventy-five counties gained population, and those were the ones where defense industries were located. Overall, the state lost enough people between 1940 and 1950 to cost it one seat in the United States House of Representatives. The shortage of agricultural labor in the state was so acute during the war that local governments in predominantly agricultural areas resorted to unusual, if not illegal, tactics. In the summer of 1942, the small eastern Arkansas city of Harrisburg began to strictly enforce its vagrancy laws in order to force the few unemployed but able-bodied men to find work. The mayor of nearby Marked Tree issued a work-or-jail edict for the same purpose. Declaring that "this is a war age" and that every man in the city between the ages of 18 and 25 was technically a soldier, the mayor ordered the arrest of all idlers. More often than not, city officials in small agriculturally dependent towns were also planters who used their elected positions to secure labor for their business enterprises. This was illustrated by a sequel to the Marked Tree mayor's declaration. His cotton compress which had been forced to close due to a shortage of labor was suddenly reopened with a full crew of workers.[29]

Help Wanted: Men, Women, and Children

The movement of war industries into Arkansas between 1940 and 1945 created new employment opportunities for many of those who had been kept at the lower end of the wage scale or out of the labor market altogether. Some of those who benefited from the labor shortage were handicapped, youths, blacks, and women. The demand for labor was so great by the fall of 1942 that Ed McDonald, regional director of the War Manpower Commission for Arkansas, Missouri, and Oklahoma, told employers in his region that they had to "begin now—not tomorrow" to use these groups.[30] Following McDonald's order, a north Arkansas official for the United States Employment Service (USES) reported the placement of a one-legged man on a construction project after having failed to find him employment on six previous attempts. A south Arkansas USES official reported a similar case involving a black handicapped man who was previously denied employment. By January 1943, USES officials in Arkansas reported that more than one thousand physically handicapped people had been employed in the state. Employers reported that most of them made excellent workers.[31] To the physically handicapped, the war not only meant new employment opportunities and economic independence, it also brought a feeling of self-pride and individual worth. Public acceptance of the handicapped was also enhanced with the realization that they too were doing their part to help win the war.

Just as Arkansas' handicapped were given an opportunity to serve the nation during the war, so too was its youth. Before youths in Arkansas under sixteen years of age could work full-time, they were required to have a state-issued work permit. During the 1941–1942 fiscal year, 816 such permits were issued to minors, an increase of 324 over the previous year. Undoubtedly, there were hundreds more employed than statistics revealed since Labor Commissioner W. J. Cain cautioned the public not to take the figures literally because they did not reflect the number of youths hired illegally.[32] Employers in the private sector, desperate for labor of any kind and apparently with state acquiescence, simply ignored the age requirement for full-time employees and hired minors to compensate for the shortage of adult labor. Arkansas did not keep a record of the number of youths over age sixteen who were employed on a full-time basis, but there were thousands who dropped out of school and voluntarily joined the labor force. Youths of all ages gained valuable work experience as well as immediate monetary gains, but their ability to be successful competitors in the job market of the postwar era was severely impaired by the wartime interruption of their education.

Perhaps the greatest beneficiaries of the new employment opportunities both immediately and in the long-run were women. Many women in Arkansas, especially those in the professions, realized that war would place a heavy burden on the state's manpower and eventually create new openings for women, and when those new jobs materialized they wanted to be in an advantageous position. With that in mind, the Little Rock chapter of the National Association of Business and Professional Women's Clubs (BPWC), in March 1940, endorsed a plank which had been drafted by the national organization and submitted to the two major political parties for inclusion in their 1940 platforms. It read: "The right to work for compensation shall not be abridged or denied by reason of race, religion, sex, or marital status."

There was good reason in Arkansas for supporting a "right to work" law for women, because Louisiana and twenty-three other states had passed legislation in 1939 and 1940 that restricted the right of married women to work.[33] Arkansas was a state with a strong family tradition in which the role of women was generally limited to the home and to the rearing of children. The majority of women in Arkansas accepted that role with little or no complaint. Therefore, the state chapter of the BPWC realized that if the Arkansas legislature followed the example of Louisiana and other states, it would probably have the support of a large segment of the state's female population. Letters to the editors of state newspapers on the issue were revealing. One Arkansas woman said that she believed that working women, especially working mothers, were the cause of crime in the streets. "Put the women in the homes where God intended us to be," she declared, "and just watch our boys get a break." Another said that "the menace in this country is the 'hog' in business, married women with supporting husbands."[34] It was the desire to counter this attitude that caused the Little Rock chapter of the BPWC to endorse enthusiastically a national "right to work" law for women. Unfortunately for those who wanted to confine women to the home, especially married ones, the demands of a nation at war would not bypass any segment of its population.

There was little demand for women workers during the early stages of the national defense program, because most jobs were in construction, rather than in production where the skills of women could best be utilized. In June of 1940, the percentage of women in the nation's labor force was approximately 13.9 percent, the same that it had been in 1910. But after 1941, the percentage of women in the labor force increased dramatically. By the summer of 1943, 31 percent of the workers in the national labor force were women, and they were 20 percent of the state workers.[35] The percentage of women in Arkansas' labor force did not meet the national average, because the state had fewer defense industries in which most of the women were employed. Arkansas only received 1.16 percent of the federal defense dollar.[36] But Arkansas women were heavily recruited by the defense industries that did locate in the state. An ad for women workers for the Arkansas Ordnance Plant in Jacksonville read: "If you are a woman with long, slender, sensitive hands that are nimble and sure-fingered, you are needed at the Arkansas Ordnance Plant, Jacksonville." To those who decried the employment of married women, the war industries appeared to be the old deluder in disguise, because it was those women that they wanted most. An *Arkansas Gazette* feature story on munition workers said that personnel directors at the defense industries where munitions were made favored happily married women over single ones. Satisfactory home life, according to employers, was conducive to the calm mental attitude required for assembly line workers who made fuses, detonators, boosters, and primers for the weapons of the armed forces.[37]

The wartime munitions industries in Arkansas were not the only employers of large numbers of women. They were also called upon to fill jobs vacated by men in radio operations, aircraft riveting, sheet metal work, machine shop employment, woodwork, drafting, and agricultural operations and management. In April 1942, women in Arkansas began training as aircraft riveters, and in May the first class graduated. These women, however, were forced to leave Arkansas, because there was no state aircraft manufacturing industry. Others who received training in specific skills remained in the state. This was especially true in agricultural operations and management. A typical example was the mother of the Patrick Lambert family of the Amity community in Clark County. While the men were away working in the war industries, the women—Mrs. Lambert and her four daughters, ranging in age from eleven to seventeen—took care of the family farm. They harvested four loads of hay, ten wagonloads of corn, seventy-five bushels of potatoes, canned seven hundred quarts of food, and did all of the planting and plowing.[38] To acquire the skills required to successfully operate farm machinery, women like the Lamberts enrolled in a national "tractorette" training program sponsored by the International Harvester Company. They were taught how to operate, service, and repair farm machinery. Women also proved to be valuable and competent additions to private industry hard hit by the manpower shortage. It was a common sight by 1943 to see women working as bank tellers, newspaper reporters, press operators, cab and bus drivers, and as mechanics in automobile repair shops. "The few men left in the ranks of private industry during the war," commented one observer, "walked around looking startled, scared, and funny." But there were few complaints from employers about the job performance of their female employees.[39]

By 1943 so many Arkansas women had moved into the labor market, leaving homes and children unattended, that state labor commissioner W. J. Cain, requested that the legislature limit their working hours. State labor laws in 1943, established by Act 70 of 1937, allowed women employed by private industry to work a maximum of fifty-four hours per week. The limit on working hours applied only to private industry, and did not apply to women employees of the state who often worked twelve to thirteen hours per day, six days per week, for a monthly salary of $35 to $40 plus room and board. The state was allowed to work women in excess of the fifty-four limit because, according to the state supreme court, women employees of the state were not specifically mentioned when the 1937 statute was enacted. Needless to say, women rapidly abandoned low-paying state jobs for employment in the war industries where they could earn up to 60¢ per hour while working an eight to ten hour day. In 1943 the state legislature, acting on Cain's request, passed House Bill 104. This law kept the fifty-four hours per week limit on working women, including women employed by the state, and required employers, in certain industries—domestic help was exempt—to pay time-and-a-half for all hours worked above forty-eight. It was hoped that the new law would prevent women from leaving state jobs for more lucrative ones in the war industries and discourage private employers from working women excessively long hours. And state social workers, who supported the legislation, hoped that the new law would allow mothers to spend more time at home with their young children and thereby curb growing wartime juvenile delinquency.[40]

As Arkansas women marched off to jobs, few complained about the long hours and the extended absences from home and family. But there was a noticeable change in their attitudes and appearance. A foreman in one of the state's largest war industries that had formerly employed all-male crews complained that the new women employees were harder to handle than men because "they can't be bossed but have to be persuaded."[41] As for their appearance, it became commonplace to see women in overalls, khakis, and street slacks. Generally, the conservative Arkansas public approved of women wearing pants on the job, especially if their jobs called for the free use of arms and legs, but it was reluctant to place its stamp of approval on wearing them after working hours. "Slacks are definitely not for the streets," declared the women's fashion editor of the *Arkansas Gazette*. The editor urged women to limit their wearing of slacks to work and to their proper place in women's sports. Similar sentiments were expressed by the fashion editor of the *Pine Bluff Commercial* who told women who wore slacks as part of their evening apparel that "the wearing of slacks on the streets with high-heeled, open-toed shoes and fur coats was an incongruous combination." A survey of men questioned about women wearing slacks after working hours revealed that the majority disapproved. Women were even more likely to be critical.[42]

Arkansas was a socially conservative state during the 1940s and women were one of its more conservative elements. Some wrote letters to the editors of their local newspapers to express their distaste for the new styles in women's clothing. Typical was a verse published by the *Arkansas Gazette:*

No woman who can buy a mirror
and see herself as others see her
just see herself before and aft
and realize that people laughed,
would ever wear those sloppy slacks
which hike in fronts and sag in backs.
Or e'er expose those scrawny pegs
by wearing shorts, unless their legs
were fashioned like a movie star's
free from hairs and spots and scars.
So let's forget the slacks and shorts
unless they be the last resorts.
And emulate our mothers good
by dressing as we women should.[43]

Such conservative voices, however, appeared to have had little impact on working women who continued to wear pants, both on and off the job, in ever increasing numbers.

The results of the massive movement of Arkansas women into new wartime roles were not all positive. Working women found economic independence and greater public appreciation, but many women were not able to adjust successfully to their new roles. In 1945, near the end of the war, Mrs. Lewis S. Talley, president of the Arkansas Women's Christian Temperance Union, reported that Federal Bureau of Investigation figures showed that the number of women arrested in Arkansas on drunkenness charges was five times greater than it had been in 1932, the last year of prohibition. State statistics also showed that the number of divorces granted during the war far outnumbered marriages. The divorce rate in the defense centers was extremely high. In El Dorado, which had a number of defense plants that employed large numbers of women, forty-one divorces were granted on a single day in May of 1943. In Pulaski County, where the state capital, several war industries, and Camp Robinson were located, the Domestic Relations Department of Little Rock's Chancery Court approved 2,112 of 2,572 divorce applications in 1944 alone. The tragedy of the growing divorce rate, according to chancery court officials, was that the majority of the divorces were granted not to young couples who had hastily married during the war but to older couples who could not adjust to the stress of wartime conditions.[44] One of the unanswered questions raised by the wartime employment of women was, "Were the benefits of full employment and economic independence worth the cost?"

Working women during World War II played a major role in keeping Arkansas industries, businesses, and farms operating at full capacity. Occupying center stage, they were both scorned and admired for their ability to accept and execute new responsibilities while ordinary mothers and homemakers went unnoticed while they performed the important societal function of maintaining traditional family stability. Ruth Millett, a staff writer for the *Pine Bluff Commercial,* pleaded their cause when she called upon the public to "let's not forget the women who are busy doing woman's work—having babies and taking care of them. It isn't a spectacular job they are performing—but it is the most important job a woman can do." [45] It was a job that many Arkansas women preferred since the majority of them voluntarily returned to their traditional roles after the war.

The entry of the United States into World War II proved to be a financial windfall for Arkansas and its people. Jobs were plentiful; all who wanted to work could easily find employment. The problem of a surplus rural farm population which was largely unemployed in 1939 was quickly eliminated by the wartime demand for skilled and unskilled labor. Between 1939 and 1943, the dollar income of all industrial employees in Arkansas rose 61.3 percent, from $831 to $1,340. In the war industries, incomes rose 98.3 percent, from $945 in 1940 to $1,874 in 1943. [46] Higher wages held steady for the duration of the war. Women, children, minorities, and the handicapped found new and exciting work which brought them a degree of economic independence and self-fulfillment. But the economic gains of Arkansas citizens during the turbulent years of World War II were achieved under stress and placed a severe strain on their personal and social lives.

3 The Social Impact of War

The inauguration of the nation's defense program in 1940 and the entry of the United States into the Second World War in 1941 brought prosperity to depression-riddled Arkansas. Unemployment, the scourge of the 1930s, quickly became a bad memory; jobs were plentiful and business was booming. Jobs lasted for the duration of the war, but the spending spree generated by full employment was short-lived. Wartime demands for agricultural and industrial products created severe shortages on the home front caused in part by a government rationing program that was designed to make sure that necessary supplies reached the nation's armed forces abroad and those of our allies. The spending boom on consumer goods that had characterized the early stages of the national defense program and the first few months of the war was suddenly halted by rationing. Domestic automobile production was sharply curtailed; gasoline, tires, sugar, meat, and numerous other consumer goods were rationed. Even the simplest routines of home and family life were disrupted by directives emanating from the War Production Board, the Office of Production Management, and a myriad of other federal regulatory agencies.

The Economic and Social Impact of Wartime Rationing

The rationing of gasoline and tires evoked a vigorous protest in rural Arkansas. Farmers who were being encouraged to increase food production could not understand why fuel and tires for farm use were being restricted. They were especially perturbed over a requirement calling for rationing forms to be distributed through county courthouses. The travel involved cost them valuable time during the planting and harvest season. The Arkansas Farm Bureau, representing the state's large agricultural interests, campaigned for the exemption of gasoline, especially diesel fuel that was essential for tractor operation. The bureau also wanted local community agencies, rather than county courthouses, to be in charge of tire and gasoline rationing, believing that community control of rationing would ensure farmers an adequate supply without unnecessary delays and the problems of government red tape.[1]

The fears that the rationing of tires and gasoline would slow the production of foodstuffs and hurt the agricultural economy of Arkansas proved to be groundless. Small farmers benefited greatly from the demand for increased food production. At the beginning of the war there were 253,013 farms in Arkansas with a combined population of 667,000 persons, 62 percent of whom were sharecroppers and tenants. Few of these grew their own food supply. In 1940, according to a survey of food production on Arkansas farms by the Department of Agriculture at the University of Arkansas, 55,000 families had no milch cows; 22,000 had no chickens; 68,000 raised no pork; and only 60,000 had gardens. During the war some of the small farms were abandoned, but many of those who remained on the farm enrolled in the government's Food-For-Victory program diversified their operations, and significantly increased food production. The program began in January 1941, and a year later 216,000 of the state's 253,013 farm families had enrolled in the program.[2] Because of food production, the per capita income of farmers increased from $246 in 1939 to $512 by 1943.[3] Obviously, these farmers suffered no major setbacks or delays because of gasoline and tire rationing. The Food-For-Victory program succeeded because of farmers' desire to do their part to support the war effort, and the urge to take advantage of higher prices paid for agricultural products.

To complement the Food-For-Victory program on the farms, city residents were encouraged to grow victory gardens. To impress upon Arkansas the importance of the food program, Governor Homer Adkins, declaring that "food raised in the cities and towns would not only aid servicemen overseas but would also save tires and gasoline required for trucking such products to market," issued a proclamation setting aside February 8, 1943, as "Victory Garden Day" in Arkansas. For those urbanites without lawns or backyards to convert into gardens, cities across the state set aside vacant lots for those who wanted to grow their own food. The space was free, and the potential gardener only had to provide manpower, tools, and seed. Many of the available lots were converted into victory gardens by patriotic citizens, but by the summer of 1944, the gardening boom had fizzled. The public, complained Aubrey D. Gates, associate director of the University of Arkansas Agricultural Extension Service, had developed a complacent attitude about the food program because they believed the nation's supply to be secure. Complacency, however, was not the major reason why urbanites abandoned the victory garden program. Many of the city lots offered for gardening were covered with thick bermuda grass requiring a great deal of human muscle, time, and spade work to make them productive.[4] Since most city dwellers worked ten to twelve hours per day in the war industries or on other civilian jobs, there was little time or energy left at the end of the day for gardening.

During the first months of the war food was plentiful and prices were of little concern to well-paid workers. But by March 1942, food supplies were dwindling and the government instituted the food rationing program. Vegetables remained readily available to those who grew victory gardens or who cared to travel to nearby farms for their supply, but the rationing of meats hurt both urban and rural dwellers. By December 1942, lard (shortening) and salt meat, the kitchen standbys for thousands of families in all socioeconomic groups, became unobtainable in many sections of the state and in very short supply elsewhere. Supplies were so scarce in the heavily populated defense centers that workers threatened to quit their jobs unless they got some fats for cooking.[5] Adequate supplies, however, were simply not available, and urban workers were forced to use their imaginations and creative abilities to come up with acceptable substitutes for quality meats and other rationed food products.

Pig ears were one of the most popular items used as a substitute for salt pork by urban industrial workers and middle-class Arkansans. Pig ears, however, were by no means a new or unusual item on the menu—poor whites and blacks had been eating them for decades, along with pig's feet, chitterlings, and other pork cast-offs that were considered inedible by the state's middle and upper-middle classes—but they achieved a new appreciation among those groups as they were eagerly sought for seasoning when cooking turnip and mustard greens, dried beans, and lentils. Meat rationing also made frogs a popular substitute. Frogs were unrationed and sold for 60¢ per pound (about five mature frogs). Little Rock grocers reported that it was not just frog legs that customers were seeking: they wanted the whole frog, which was usually chicken-fried.

Using their ingenuity, citizens were able to compensate for inadequate supplies of gasoline, tires, and quality foodstuffs, but they could find no substitute for the loss of doctors, nurses, and other medical personnel.[6] The state had always suffered from a shortage of doctors and nurses. In 1941 there was only one doctor in the state for every 1,500 residents, and the number of doctors decreased as the armed forces called physicians into the services. Arkansans of all ages suffered from poor health, but the physical condition of the state's youth was particularly deplorable. In 1940, Dr. W. B. Grayson, director of the state health department, reported that 90 percent of all school children examined by the department had some type of physical defect and that 50 percent of them were major health problems. This was clearly revealed by selective service physical examinations. In 1943, the Arkansas State Dental Association and the State Board of Health jointly reported that 35 percent of Arkansans rejected by the armed forces were turned down because of diseased teeth and defective eyesight. They also reported that pellagra, rickets, and obesity, all caused by poor nutrition, were frequently encountered. In view of the fact that Arkansas was an agricultural state and that few of its farmers grew part of their own food supply, it is amazing that the rejection rate of Arkansas by the armed services was as low as it was.[7]

Not only did Arkansas lose part of its critically short supply of doctors during the war, it also lost a large percentage of its nurses. Between 1941 and 1943, the state furnished the armed forces with five times its quota of trained nurses, and by 1944 it had fewer nurses per capita than any other state. In the summer of 1944, the State Council for the War Nursing Service reported that there were only 653 registered nurses working in Arkansas, a ration of 57.75 nurses for every 100,000 civilians. Although the majority of the state's nurses left their state jobs for military service, many others took advantage of the home front demands for nurses and left for better paying jobs in other states. Even if the state had been able to keep an adequate supply of doctors and nurses, it did not have sufficient medical facilities needed for patient care. Arkansas' civilian wartime population was over 1,800,000, but there were only 2,858 beds in state approved hospitals. The lack of facilities probably accounts for the shortage of doctors in Arkansas prior to World War II, and the shortage of doctors undoubtedly contributed to the health problems of the state's population. The loss of doctors and nurses during the war simply aggravated a critical problem which already existed.[8]

The poor were especially victimized. Arkansas was sparsely populated, and outside the few urban areas families lived far apart from one another and even farther from city hospitals and clinics. Since most of the rural poor could not afford the cost of transportation to medical facilities, the state welfare department regularly sent agents into homes throughout the state's seventy-five counties to attend to health care needs. But because of the government's decision to ration tires and gasoline, state Welfare Commissioner John G. Pipkin ordered all social workers in the state to reduce travel by 50 percent. The majority of the 260 cars used by the 250 county directors, supervisors, and advisory personnel to administer health care to the poor were privately owned, but their travel expenses were paid by the state. Pipkin's order cut these services by one-half. This was followed by a directive from J. H. Carter of the state banking department's security division ordering funeral homes in the state to end free ambulance service, a practice begun in the late 1930s by an enterprising undertaker who agreed to transport a mother and her first-born home from the hospital free of charge. Competition between operators grew until free ambulance service was taken as a matter of course. According to Carter's directive, "such service of any other free merchandise would be considered a violation of state and federal rationing laws." Pipkin's and Carter's directives denied Arkansas' poor badly needed health care and transportation services that only the state could afford to provide.[9]

Some of the hardships caused by the federal rationing program were unavoidable; others, however, were unnecessary, such as the rationing of sliced bread. In January 1943, the Office of Price Administration (OPA), in order to help control spiraling food costs, inaugurated the brief but devastating "Battle of the Bread Loaf" when it announced that sliced bread would no longer be available to the public. The pre-breakfast hour in the kitchen, a madhouse at best for working parents, suddenly became a panic-stricken, blood-letting miniature war zone as mothers and fathers mutilated thumbs and wrists in an attempt to provide their crying children with sliced bread. Probably nothing during the war came as close to sending homemakers into the streets as did the bread directive. Consistent complaints forced the OPA to lift the ban in March 1943.[10] It had lasted only three months, but its repeal represented only a minor concession to a people who were being continually asked to make sacrifices for a nation at war.

Undoubtedly the rationing program caused some inconveniences, but many saw it as a positive good. Wives and sweethearts were quite pleased with the rationing of tires and gasoline since it resulted in their loved ones spending more time with them. As one newspaper editor succinctly put it:

> He used to call her honey, then he switched to "sugar" when that sweet product became scarce. As time went on he assured her that she was his "brand new rubber tire" and that her eyes were like "two cups of good coffee." And now his love is in full bloom as he fervidly declares that she looks better to him than a full tank of gasoline.

Others, not as poetic as the newsman, also saw a positive side to rationing. "The shortage of tires and gasoline," wrote one astute observer in Arkansas, "keeps people home and gives them the opportunity to get acquainted with not only neighbors but members of their own families. The shortage of consumer products and full employment gave people the opportunity to get out of debt, purchase war bonds, and save for the day when consumer products will again be available." [11] It was war; jobs were plentiful and wages were good. People had money to spend, but there was little to buy.

Public Education: A Struggle for Survival

Although the war brought a return of economic prosperity to Arkansas, little of the increased income found its way into the coffers of the state's public schools. Public education was financed almost entirely from revenues generated by state, personal property, and real estate taxes. In 1934, a special session of the legislature had seriously eroded the tax base for public education by reducing real estate tax rates by two-thirds in order to relieve the economic burdens of property owners. In the year prior to that session, funding for public education in Arkansas had averaged only $2.90 per pupil. Thus the action of the legislature in 1934 was devastating. The public schools were able to remain open on a one million dollar appropriation to the state's schools for the 1933–1934 academic year by the Works Project Administration (WPA) in 1933. [12] The WPA, however, believed that funding for public education was the responsibility of the state and threatened to cut off all aid if the 1935 legislature did not increase its support for public education. The loss of federal dollars by the state's public schools would have meant certain collapse. When the 1935 general assembly convened in January, funding for public education was the principal issue. "If that one problem can be satisfactorily solved," commented one legislator, "it will be a successful session." After heated debate, and over the opposition of planters from eastern Arkansas, the legislature passed a two-percent retail sales tax. The tax was on all commodities except specified food and medicine. Of the $2,250,000 the tax was expected to generate, $1,500,000 was earmarked for public education. However, the sales tax did not create sufficient revenues because the legislature refused to restore the property tax base that it had reduced during the 1934 special session, and because the governor and other state leaders believed that public education beyond the primary grades was the responsibility of the counties. No real effort was made by state officials to secure adequate funds for public education, and when the legislature convened for its biennial session in 1937, little was done to increase support for public education. Thus, Arkansas public schools entered the era of World War II operating at pre-depression funding levels. [13]

When defense industries began to move into the state in early 1940, public schools located in or near the areas were not prepared, physically or financially, to handle the influx of new students. The cities of Hope and Fort Smith illustrate the problems faced by school districts in defense areas. Hope was the site of the army's Southwestern Proving Grounds and its population, between January 1940 and January 1942, increased from 7,475 to 15,475. In Fort Smith, where Fort Chaffee and a large aluminum plant were located, the population increased by 3,600 between June 1940 and August 1941. Of the latter there were 1,500 defense workers, with wives and children totalling an additional 2,100. Public schools in Hope and Fort Smith, like their counterparts in other defense centers in Arkansas, were unable to accommodate the new students and turned to the state for help, but assistance was not forthcoming. In 1940, when the defense industries first began moving into Arkansas and the schools began to experience severe shortages in facilities and personnel, Ralph Jones, state commissioner of education, informed public school administrators not to expect relief from the state because the school equalizing fund was already operating at a $350,000 deficit.[14] This fund had been established in the 1930s to make sure that school districts had a minimum operating budget. Under the program if local funds did not guarantee minimum needs, the state would make up the difference. However, the state could not fulfill its responsibilities because it refused to restore the pre-1934 tax base, and the legislature was unwilling to levy other taxes for the benefit of public education.

The legislature also refused to increase teacher salaries so that the public schools could compete with the rapidly growing war industries for qualified personnel. For the 1939–1940 academic year the average monthly teacher salary in Arkansas was $57.83 for white teachers and $31.12 for blacks.[15] Consequently, teachers began to abandon their positions in the public schools for better paying industrial jobs. When Commissioner Ralph Jones asked the 1940 legislature to remedy the situation, he reported that he was told to quit complaining because "we were better off than farmers and that we were being paid as much as we had a right to expect." The legislature was controlled by the state's large agricultural interests from eastern Arkansas, and they had never looked favorably on expenditures for public education. Faced with this negative attitude, it was no wonder that many teachers in the state left their jobs for better paying ones elsewhere. In the 1941–1942 academic year, forty public schools failed to open their doors and seventy-five more were forced to close after only two months of operation due to teacher shortages. When the schools opened for the fall term in 1942, only 54 percent of the state's white public school teachers reported for work, representing a turnover of 46 percent compared to the normal 28.6 percent. Although no figures were given, Commissioner Jones said similar conditions existed in the state's black schools.

In the 1939–1940 academic year, the average teacher salary for all of the state's teachers, black and white combined, was $750 per year which did not significantly change by 1943. By comparison, jobs in defense industries averaged between $160 and $200 per month.[16] The inability of public schools to pay competitive salaries created a critical teacher shortage by 1943.

Although there was nearly full employment during the war, school districts did not benefit from the increased income because the legislature refused to raise taxes for public education and because local districts could not raise school millage rates without voter approval. Attempts to increase local revenue failed because Arkansans in general did not place a very high value on public education and because many of the voters in the defense centers, where the demand for teachers and facilities was crucial, refused to support increased taxation to pay for the education of children whose parents they viewed as "outsiders." Few of the defense workers were registered to vote in the areas where they were employed. Therefore, local revenues for public education increased little during World War II. For the 1942–1943 school year, 1,396 of Arkansas' 2,345 school districts collected only $100 in local revenues, and there was no increase in revenues for the remaining districts.[17] Also, there is little evidence that state and local authorities made a determined effort to collect delinquent taxes.

The quality of prewar public education in Arkansas was poor. In 1940 there were 13,173 employed teachers in the state of whom 2,840, or 22.3 percent, had less than one year of college training, and those most qualified were the first to leave the profession. The teacher shortage was so acute that the state Department of Education was forced to grant emergency teaching permits to recent high school graduates who had neither college credits nor teaching experience. Before the end of the 1943–1944 academic year, so many teachers had left their profession that many school districts began raiding their neighbors for personnel. "Teacher pirating" had become so common by 1943 that frustrated school administrators appealed to the legislature to halt the practice. Officials responded by rejecting legislation that would have increased teacher salaries to competitive levels, passing instead a statute forbidding school districts to hire teachers from another district before the expiration of their contracts.[18] The new contract law, however, did little to stabilize the teaching profession, because most of the teachers who broke their contracts went to work in war-related industries rather than other school districts.

Recognizing that many small towns would explode into boom towns with the establishment of factories and camps, Congress passed the Community Facilities (Lanham) Act in 1940. Under this law 2,800 child care centers were constructed throughout the nation, but few were built in Arkansas, and the Lanham Act did little to alleviate the distress of the public schools. The situation became increasingly desperate, and school administrators sought other forms of federal assistance.[19]

In 1943, senators Lister Hill of Alabama and John W. E. Thomas of Oklahoma, reacting to the pleas for aid from financially distressed school districts, introduced in Congress a federal aid-to-education proposal. The Hill-Thomas Bill authorized annual federal appropriations of $200 million during the war to supplement state funds for the payment of teacher salaries. An additional $100 million was to be appropriated for the equalization of educational opportunities in the states. The $200 million was to be distributed to the states on the basis of pupil enrollment and the $100 million on the basis of financial need. Educators in Arkansas urged their congressmen to support the bill. Declaring that "if we are stopped now for lack of funds, by next year we will be going on all fours," Forrest Rozzell, field representative of the Arkansas Education Association (AEA), urged members to write their congressmen in support of the federal education bill.[20] In addition to Rozzell, the majority of educators in Arkansas felt that federal aid for public education, especially the Hill-Thomas Bill, was the answer to their problems.

Whereas educators saw the Hill-Thomas Bill as a panacea for the public school system, state political and business leaders viewed it as a dangerous intrusion on "states rights." They believed that the bill would increase taxes and lead to a federal takeover of public schools, denying parents and taxpayers control of local institutions that were vital to their interest. However, it was not the threat of federal control of public education that critics of the Hill-Thomas Bill feared the most; rather, it was the fear that federal aid to public education might lead to the repeal of the Jim Crow laws that governed public schools in the state. That was the concealed message from the editor of the *Arkansas Gazette,* J. N. Heiskell, in an editorial entitled "When Southern School Forces Urge Federal School Aid." Educators in Arkansas and throughout the South were urged to reject federal aid because "public education in the South is complicated by special human and social problems that exist only in minor degrees, or not at all, in other parts of the country."[21] Critics of federal aid to public education appeared to be more interested in the maintenance of racial segregation than they were in quality education for all public school students.

An attack on southern racism in education materialized when Senator William Langer of North Dakota succeeded in getting an amendment attached to the Hill-Thomas Bill that prohibited discrimination in the benefits and appropriations under the bill "or in state funds supplements thereby on account of race, creed, or color." [22] Southerners, the greatest supporters of the original bill, were now faced with a dilemma. They could either support the amended bill or vote to have it committed to the Senate Education Committee. The choice was not a difficult one for Arkansas senators. They realized that the amended bill, if passed, would force their state—which in 1943 was spending $25 on each white student in the public schools compared to $10 for each black—to equalize both funding and teacher salaries. In the 1941–1942 academic year, the average salary paid black teachers in Arkansas was $267 compared to $625 for white teachers. [23] Faced with the choice of voting to equalize educational opportunities and salaries for all of the state's teachers and students or denying them equality in order to preserve segregation, Arkansas senators voted with their southern counterparts to have the Hill-Thomas Bill recommitted to the Senate Education Committee from which it never again emerged.

Commenting on his vote to recommit, Junior Senator John L. McClellan said that the Langer amendment had been added "forcing amalgamation of the white and Negro schools in the nation. With that amendment in there I couldn't vote for the bill without voting to sacrifice our dual education in the South, segregating white and Negro races." Senator McClellan's views were shared by educational leaders in his state. Ralph Jones, commissioner of education, said that he and the state education department were opposed to the amended version of the bill and to any bill "that required states to divide funds between races on an equal basis." Forrest Rozzell of the AEA, who was one of the more outspoken supporters of the original federal aid bill, also opposed the amended version and was pleased by its defeat, although he still felt that federal aid could solve the problems of the state's public schools. "We want federal aid," commented Rozzell, "but we want it in a form that will allocate money without discretionary powers allotted to any federal office." It was somewhat ironic that while the Senate debated the Hill-Thomas Bill, the United States was fighting a world war in defense of racial equality and equal opportunity. On the home front Arkansas, and southerners in general, revealed a dogged determination to preserve inequity. [24]

After southern racism had prevented Congress from passing federal legislation to aid the nation's public schools in 1943, the *Arkansas Democrat*, which had also been a critic of federal aid, joined forces with the AEA and called upon the legislature to increase the state sales tax from two to three cents per dollar in order to improve financing for public schools. It also recommended that the state improve the system of assessing and collecting real estate and personal property taxes which generated the bulk of public school revenues. But when the legislature met in January 1945, it refused to increase the funding. At the annual fall meeting of the AEA in 1945, Governor Ben Laney told the teachers that more money would not solve the state's educational problems. "Only by increasing the producing and consuming power of the individual . . . can the economic status of Arkansas be raised, and with it the power to develop and support public schools." The governor seemed oblivious to the fact that it took well-trained minds to improve the economic and productive capabilities of Arkansans and that the state's youth were not getting that training in the poorly financed public school system.[25]

As the schools prepared for the 1945–1946 academic year, the future of public education in the state did not look promising. Over 50 percent of the prewar teaching staff had left the profession, and 72 percent of the replacements had completed less than twelve semester hours of college work. The relaxation of educational requirements for public school teachers had not solved the problem of teacher shortages. After two months of operation the schools still needed 1,000 teachers.[26] Student attendance was also far below prewar levels. During the 1942–1943 academic year, 100,000 of the state's 170,000 youths between the ages of 13 and 18 failed to attend school because teachers were not available. The shortage of teachers combined with poor funding forced many rural school districts to consolidate. Between 1941 and 1945, the state's 3,009 independent school districts were reduced to 2,345. Consolidation, however, did little to improve the overall quality of education since 1,900 of the remaining districts lacked the funds needed to provide a minimum accredited high school education, nor did it increase attendance. Those districts that began the 1945–1946 academic year averaged only 123.2 pupil attendance days per year, compared to a southern states' average of 138.6 and a national average of 149.6.[27] Public school officials felt that after the war teachers and students would return to the classrooms, but many teachers who had left their positions in the public schools for other jobs did not return and left Arkansas for better paying careers elsewhere.

World War II posed major difficulties for public schools throughout the nation. In rural states the problems took on added dimensions as defense industries moved into small cities and flooded the schools with the children of employees. In Arkansas the understaffed and poorly financed public schools could not meet the needs of the new pupils, and many of them were turned away because teachers and facilities were unavailable. Many of those without access to public schools took jobs in the defense industries and the private sector where their labor was in demand. Between 1940 and 1941, the number of working teen-agers in the nation rose from one to three million.[28] In Arkansas, no statistics were kept for youths employed full-time over age sixteen, because they were not required to have state-issued work permits. But the state issued 816 permits for those under sixteen for the 1941–1942 fiscal year, and the state labor commissioner estimated that thousands more worked illegally.[29] Therefore, it would be reasonable to assume that thousands of Arkansas youths between thirteen and eighteen did not attend school and took either full or part-time jobs. They were the ones who were damaged most severely by the wartime crisis. However, many of the educational difficulties in Arkansas that surfaced during the war years were not war-induced but were problems that grew out of a general disregard for public education and were merely aggravated by war. They were not insurmountable, but their solution required forceful and dynamic leadership, qualities lacking in the state during the critical war years.

Diluting an Institution: The Social Impact of World War II on the Arkansas Family

At the onset of World War II most Arkansans still believed in the Victorian family ideal: a strong, provident father faithfully supported by a devoted wife whose dominion was the home and who bore the responsibilities of raising the children. There was entrenched sentiment to continue the tradition despite demands made upon the state's women by the war. Although there was little opposition to single women entering the labor force to replace men who had joined the armed forces or who had taken new jobs in the rapidly growing war industries, the attitude toward married women with families was quite different, since they were perceived as the foundation of a stable family structure and an orderly society. Thus, many felt the movement of women from the home to full employment could only result in family deterioration and social chaos.

The first and most obvious sign of family decay was the rapid growth of juvenile delinquency, especially among young girls. The rising delinquency rate was accompanied by a tremendous increase in the number of reported cases of venereal disease. Social diseases, as they were politely called by many, had always been a problem and reached crisis proportions during the war. In January 1940, Governor Carl E. Bailey, in a proclamation designating February 1, 1940, as "Social Hygiene Day," declared that venereal disease was the state's number one health problem.[30]

In Jonesboro, the Craighead County health department issued a warning linking disease with the ability of American soldiers to defend the nation. A notice printed in the local paper in bold type read: "OUR TOWN—THE FRONT LINE OF VENEREAL DISEASE DEFENSE." The message beneath the headline urged the public to be on guard against infection because "America's soldiers form the nation's first line of defense . . . and that a syphilitic soldier is a wounded soldier." The rapid growth in such cases was not limited to Craighead County, for practically all communities in the state that contained war industries or military bases were faced with the same phenomenon. Craighead County published its warning in February 1941, and by July the venereal disease rate in Little Rock was so high that the city council passed an ordinance giving the health department authority to detain and examine persons believed to be suffering from such "social diseases." In Fort Smith, the growth in reported cases was so alarming that Circuit Judge J. Sam Woods called for a grand jury investigation.[31]

A rise in the juvenile delinquency rate accompanied the increase in venereal disease cases. In Pine Bluff, the Jefferson County Juvenile Court declared 144 youths delinquent in 1941, compared to 75 in 1940. Records also revealed that offenders were becoming younger. In Jefferson County the average age for delinquent boys in 1940 was 15.6 years and 16 years for girls, compared to 14 for boys and 15 for girls in 1941.[32] Similar data came from juvenile court records in Little Rock. In the state's largest city 88 cases of juvenile delinquency reached court dockets in 1939, 105 in 1940, 123 in 1941, and 116 for the first six months of 1942. An especially disturbing fact was that among delinquent girls, the 14-year-old category contained the most offenders.[33] The "Victory Girls"—young girls who performed "patriotic" sexual favors for men in uniform—had arrived in Arkansas.

Social workers and juvenile officers operating around army camps attributed the growth in delinquency and venereal disease among young girls to a combination of social and economic factors caused by the war. Mrs. J. Russell Henderson, chairman of the Youth Advisory Association of the Arkansas Council for Social Agencies, placed the blame there without equivocation. "This war is directly responsible for the boom in badness because children's fathers go off to war and their mothers go to work, and thus the interest of parents is diverted from the home and their children," she said.[34] The probation officer in Pine Bluff, a city which also had military bases and war industries, gave similar reasons for the "boom in badness" in Jefferson County. An editorial in the *Arkansas Gazette* blamed the growth of delinquency on the war "which has transformed our peaceful town of homes, schools, and churches into a wartime center. . . ."[35] The prediction made by critics in

1940, that the employment of married women with children would only result in family deterioration and immorality, appeared to have gained credibility by spring 1943. There was little optimism that things would improve in the future.

The number of adult professional prostitutes also increased, but it was the Victory Girls who caused the most concern. "It is not the seasoned prostitute we are interested in, it's the teen-age girl," reported Mrs. Henderson. Urging the Little Rock City Council to pass an ordinance to keep young girls off the streets, Henderson and Major W. B. Light (U.S. Army), director of venereal disease control for the United States health department in Little Rock and Hot Springs, told the councilmen that "older women were able to secure jobs in war plants, leaving jobs as waitresses, barmaids, and carhops for teen-age girls who, due to poor wages, often turned to prostitution to supplement their meager incomes." Light also told the councilmen that 55 percent of the women admitted to the Hot Springs Public Health Center had worked on jobs paying an average of seven dollars per week, and that most of those treated for venereal disease had had contact with servicemen. The Arkansas State Department of Health informed the council that for the 1943 fiscal year 12,886 cases of syphilis and 3,534 cases of gonorrhea were treated by its officials.[36] The problem was complicated by the lack of adequate laws regarding teen-age prostitution.

Arkansas had no established procedure for treating teen-agers found guilty of prostitution but not infected with venereal disease. Therefore, cities with war industries or military bases were forced to develop their own control mechanisms. The infection rate was so high around army installations that military authorities threatened to declare nearby cities off limits to their personnel unless legislation was passed to control the social disease.[37] Despite these threats local governments were reluctant to pass strong regulatory laws. In Jonesboro and Little Rock, police departments, supported by various religious and civic groups, urged the establishment of curfews to keep teen-agers off the streets. However, authorities in both cities refused. They argued that such laws would be unfair because they would be an improper interference with parental authority and would penalize the majority in order to punish the minority. Only in Hot Springs were officials willing to establish a curfew. Even then the action did not emanate from the city council but was established after the county judge, county sheriff, and juvenile court officials requested Police Commissioner Weldon Rasberry to take action. Rasberry said it was "the most drastic request that I have ever received but one that I heartily welcome because I have never seen a time when parents were so indifferent to the welfare of their children." In addition, he said many mothers were abandoning their young altogether.[38]

Before the war, the Arkansas Child Welfare Division always had sufficient foster families with which to place children from broken homes, babies of unmarried mothers, children deserted by their parents, and those placed under the division's care for delinquency. The advent of the war reversed the situation. In January 1942, the division was making, for the first time in its history, public appeals for foster homes for unattended children.[39] As these became scarce and as the reported cases of unattended children increased, more teen-agers and pre-teen juveniles were sentenced to state reformatories because there was no other place to send them. Between December 1942 and July 1943, the population of the state reformatory for white youths grew from 68 to 116. In 1944, three boys, the oldest only twelve, were sentenced to that institution after confessing to several burglaries. They told authorities that they committed the crimes because they were alone and had nothing else to do.[40] The sight of unattended boys and girls on the streets at all hours had become commonplace by the second year of the war.

Many abandoned children in urban centers were those belonging to men whose wives received from $50 to $125 per month in dependency pay from their husbands, reported officials of the Pulaski County Juvenile Court in Little Rock and Jacksonville. Similar reports came from other industrial areas. "We have encountered some strange conditions caused by servicemen's wives, who seem to have forgotten their husbands and to be trying to forget their children," read a joint statement issued by officers of the Garland County Parole Office in Hot Springs, the Red Cross, and the Public Welfare and Safety Division. Of the many cases cited by Garland County officials, one outlined the condition of three children between the ages of three and eleven who were discovered on the verge of starvation living alone in a dilapidated one-room cabin. Their mother, who was receiving a $120 per month dependency allotment, had abandoned them and was living with a female friend in a downtown Hot Springs hotel. In Little Rock, reported cases of juvenile delinquency and child abandonment reached such alarming proportions by the fall of 1943 that Judge Lawrence C. Auten, president of the Arkansas Judicial Commission (composed of circuit judges and chancellors from throughout the state), declared that the situation "threatens to 'undermine our society' unless the increase in juvenile delinquency is stopped and persons approaching the altar take a different look at the institution of marriage."[41]

Auten's concern was shared by other groups who felt that the cancer attacking the family in Arkansas could be curbed if the legislature would repeal the state's ninety-day divorce law and establish stronger premarital and divorce laws. Under the 1931 ninety-day divorce law, anyone could establish residence in Arkansas, start divorce proceedings after sixty days, and qualify for a final decree thirty days after the filing. The law required only that the defendant be notified of the proceedings after which there were six months to challenge the decree. An editorial in the *Arkansas Gazette* charged that the state's divorce law was passed by the legislature "for wholly mercenary reasons. It was an open bid for a share of the quick and easy divorce business cultivated by a few other states." The *Gazette,* which had opposed the ninety-day law since it was first adopted, called for a return to the old law which required anyone filing for a divorce in Arkansas to be a state resident for a minimum of one year.[42]

Most of the traffic in easy marriages and quick divorces took place in Arkansas counties that bordered the states of Tennessee, Missouri, and Oklahoma. In these counties marriage and divorce were big business. In Hot Springs, a national resort area close to Oklahoma, the divorce mill there ground out matrimonial separations at the rate of more than one per day in 1940. In 1941 out-of-state residents took advantage of Arkansas' ninety-day law to help set new records in the Hot Springs divorce business; 532 decrees were granted, 112 above the record set in 1940. With local officials either unable or unwilling to change matters, the state legislature came under increasing pressure from judges, social workers, concerned public officials, and religious groups to take positive action.[43]

When the legislature convened in January 1941, several members introduced legislation designed to inhibit the growth of divorce and to curb the spread of venereal disease. Representative Carroll C. Hollensworth of Bradley County introduced a bill to repeal the ninety-day divorce law by simply restoring the one-year residency requirement.[44] To help control the spread of social diseases, Representative Ben D. Brickhouse of Little Rock introduced a bill to require applicants to pass mental and venereal disease examinations administered by a licensed physician fifteen days before applying for a marriage license. Brickhouse told his colleagues that "we have done much to improve our breeds of livestock, but little has been accomplished to improve the stock of human beings. The marriage contract," he continued, "is our most sacred covenant. Our laws will not permit trial marriages, but unfortunately that is what many young people are practicing . . . they are married today and divorced tomorrow and much of it is caused by disease." In the Senate a companion bill to the Brickhouse measure was introduced by Senator George Stell of Nashville. The Hollensworth Bill was never considered by the House, but the Brickhouse-Stell proposal generated heated debate.[45]

Opposition to the bill was led by legislators from the border counties of eastern Arkansas. Representative James C. Hale of Crittenden County, located on the Tennessee border, argued that the Brickhouse Bill would abolish the county clerk's fees that his county obtained from out-of-state couples. In the Senate, Senator Ivy Crawford of Blytheville, Mississippi County, adjacent to both Tennessee and Missouri, charged that the Brickhouse-Stell people were "thirty years ahead of their time. Why it's just that in the last two years that we have gotten to where we can even talk about this subject [venereal disease]." Besides, he said, "only Negroes have syphilis" and the passage of the bill "would practically abolish marriage among Negroes." Expanding Crawford's use of racism, Senator Lawrence L. Mitchell of Prescott proclaimed that the bill was both "an insult to the white women of the state" and unnecessary. "White women know they don't have syphilis," he declared.[46] However out of touch with reality Crawford and Mitchell were on the subject of the incidence of venereal disease and its causes, their opposition to the bill helped send it to defeat.

County clerks and treasurers, represented by the Arkansas Clerks and Treasurers Association (ACTA), were also instrumental in defeating the marriage measure. They opposed the bill because they feared its passage would severely diminish the income they received from license fees. Indeed ACTA actually requested a twenty-five-cent increase in these fees.[47]

The Brickhouse-Stell marriage bill of 1941 fell before the combined strength of the border county representatives, the divorce lawyers, and ACTA. However, a tragic incident helped persuade the legislature to pass a compromise measure. A few days after the legislature defeated the Brickhouse-Stell Bill, a 16-year-old Jonesboro High School girl and her 21-year-old sweetheart were hastily married in a neighboring county. Within a few hours, the bride died of accidental gas poisoning in a tourist camp. Her death prompted the *Arkansas Gazette* to ask the legislature, "Are fees of county clerks—even the rich fees of the Crittenden County Clerk—worth such tragedies?" It then answered, "No, but it's a wonder that the legislature protects the fees of county clerks instead of the institution of marriage and the happiness of human lives."[48]

Following the *Gazette's* editorial attack, a compromise bill made its way through the legislature. Introduced by Representative R. Ellis McMillion of Greene County, the act forbade county clerks from issuing marriage licenses when either of the contracting parties was visibly under the influence of alcohol or drugs, and it raised the legal age for marriage in Arkansas from 14 to 16 for females and from 16 to 18 for males. The new law, however, did not satisfy those who demanded more stringent legislation. Meanwhile, delinquency, quick marriage, easy divorce, and venereal disease continued to escalate. In Ouachita County Chancery Court, all records for divorce were broken in 1943 when 41 divorces were granted in a single day.[49] Divorces granted in Little Rock under the 90-day law also reached new highs. In 1943 there were 2,325 divorce suits filed (1,712 white and 613 black) and 1,931 decrees granted (1,367 white and 564 black); only 216 suits were denied. For 1944, the Pulaski County Chancery Court granted 2,112 divorce decrees out of 2,572 suits filed. Some of the decrees involved young people who had made "gangplank marriages," but most divorces, according to Ruth Hale of the domestic relations department of the Pulaski County Chancery Court, were granted to older couples who could not adjust to the new economic independence created by the employment of both husband and wife and to the new and daily associations with other men and women on their jobs.[50] While the war afforded new economic and social opportunity, it also threatened the traditional family fabric.

In the summer of 1944, various civic, religious, and judicial organizations began a campaign to pressure the 1945 legislature to take positive action to curb the rapid rate of family deterioration in the state. A resolution adopted by the Northwestern District League of the Catholic Women's Union urged the legislature to "modify divorce laws to discourage the seeking and granting of divorces for trivial reasons," because "the foundation of society and of state government is dependent on the home and family." At their annual meeting in the same year, the fifty members of the Eighth Chancery Court Bar Association unanimously endorsed a resolution calling upon the 1945 legislature to require a three-day notice of intent to apply for a marriage license in writing to be filed with county clerks. Although there was no consensus for a particular law, most agreed that some corrective measures were needed.[51]

When the Fifty-fifth General Assembly convened in January 1945, several of its members were prepared to sponsor remedial legislation. Representative P. P. Alexander of Delight (Pike County) introduced a bill to reinstate the one-year residency requirement for divorce. Representative Russell Turnipseed of Sebastian County, supported by juvenile authorities from areas with military bases and war-related industries, sponsored a bill designed to curb the number of child abandonment cases in the state. Representative W. H. Abington of White County, who was also a physician, introduced a bill designed to prevent the spread of venereal disease by requiring prospective mothers to take blood tests for congenital syphilis. Abington admitted that his bill was a definite departure in the care of pregnant women but that its passage "would be a tremendous step toward reducing miscarriages, still births, and congenital syphilitic babies born to syphilitic mothers."[52]

The Turnipseed child abandonment bill, which stipulated fines ranging from $50 to $100 or one year in jail, or both, for parents who abandoned children under age 14, easily passed both houses of the legislature. But the Abington and Alexander bills ran into trouble. The Abington Bill, which had the support of the Arkansas Medical Society and the Arkansas State Department of Health, passed the House of Representatives by a narrow margin but was defeated in the Senate by the same forces which had killed the Brickhouse-Stell Bill in 1941. The Alexander Bill to repeal the state's 90-day divorce law never came to a vote after lawyers and county clerks from across the state converged on the legislature to oppose it.[53] But all was not totally lost.

Having failed to repeal the state's "quickie" divorce law and to pass tough disease control measures, the legislature accepted a compromise marriage bill introduced by Representative Leslie W. Buchanan of Nevada County, the state's only woman representative. Her bill, reflecting the position taken in the resolution endorsed earlier by the Eighth Chancery Court Bar Association, required a three-day waiting period between application for a marriage license and the actual ceremony. Supporters of the Buchanan Bill, which passed both houses with overwhelming majorities, said it would not only make marriages more difficult in Arkansas but "to a degree would remove from Arkansas the stigma of a reputation as a mecca for persons consummating impulsive, thoughtless, or 'gin' weddings."[54] To give the measure credibility, county clerks could be fined from $100 to $500 for failing to enforce the law. Yet, what appeared to be a victory for the supporters of strong marriage laws in Arkansas soon became bitter disappointment.

By requiring a three-day waiting period between application for a marriage license and marriage, the Buchanan Act may have eliminated unions consummated under the influence of alcohol, or so-called "gin weddings," but it did nothing to control the spread of venereal disease nor did it make divorces more difficult to acquire. It was, at best, a weak measure. Under its provisions no marriage could be voided even though the waiting period had not been observed, and the threat of penalty was nullified by a provision allowing county judges, clerks, and court officials to waive the three-day waiting period if they thought it necessary. The statute was further weakened by a ruling from the

Arkansas attorney general that the day on which an application for a marriage license was filed could be counted as one day of the three-day waiting period. Although the law made marriages in Arkansas more difficult for out-of-state applicants, its impact on state residents was minimal.[55] When the 1945 legislature closed in March, World War II was nearly over, but the war's impact on the structure of the traditional Arkansas family would be permanent.

4 The Home Front and Civil Liberties

During times of war there are, more often than not, unnecessary restrictions placed on civil liberties, and America during World War II was no exception. Comparatively, the civil liberties record of the United States was an admirable one, but it still fell short in some areas. Some groups and individuals suffered because they failed to support the war vigorously due to their religious and philosophical beliefs; others lost their civil rights because of historical and ethnic ties with wartime enemies. Both groups were found in Arkansas.

The Witnesses of Jehovah: In Search of Religious Freedom

The majority of those who refused to support the war effort belonged to the historic peace churches—Quaker, Mennonite, and the Church of the Brethren. Surprisingly, many members of these sects joined the armed forces as combatants and others accepted service as noncombatants and were classified by the army as conscientious objectors (COs). The Selective Service Act of 1940 identified two types of COs: (1) those willing to render noncombat military service, and (2) those unwilling to render any kind of military service.[1] Members of the historic peace churches usually applied for and were granted, without much difficulty, noncombat military status (CO). Other lesser known religious groups who rejected all forms of military service found CO status extremely difficult to obtain. This was especially true for members of the Watchtower Bible and Tract Society, commonly known as Jehovah's Witnesses.

In contrast to traditional peace church affiliates, Jehovah's Witnesses were not a well-known sect when the United States entered World War II. They were not well received by the general public in most areas of the nation. The element of the sect's beliefs that created hostility was their strict adherence to Exodus 20:4 and 13: "Thou shalt not make unto thee any graven image" and

"Thou shalt not kill." [2] Obeying this injunction literally, the sect refused to salute the United States flag or to join the armed forces in any capacity. During the war, people did not look kindly upon a group who refused to honor "Old Glory" or join the armed forces, yet who loudly proclaimed that they were willing to fight in the Battle of Armageddon, the final battle between good and evil alluded to in the Book of Revelation. [3] To the majority of Americans, Germany and Japan represented the earthly powers of evil, and the refusal of the Witnesses to help defeat them encouraged speculation that they were disloyal. From the invasion of Poland to the Battle of Britain, the Witnesses were one of the principal targets of mob violence in the United States. [4]

In rural Arkansas, where patriotism ran high and social life frequently centered around membership in veterans and other patriotic organizations, anyone who did not conform to local practices was suspected of being un-American. Some people felt it was their duty to make nonconformists publicly demonstrate their patriotism. Attempts to force Jehovah's Witnesses to display public acts of loyalty in Arkansas began with the national defense program in 1940. The signal for the attack on the sect was a United States Supreme Court decision. In *Minersville School District v. Gobitis,* the Court ruled that school children could be required to salute the flag as a condition of attendance even if their religious beliefs prohibited honoring secular symbols. [5] Many Arkansans interpreted the decision to mean that not only could the school children of Witnesses be forced to salute the flag but that adult members of the sect could also be forced to demonstrate patriotism.

An important part of the Witnesses' religious activity was the distribution of literature on city streets from door-to-door in residential areas. The literature was used to explain the sect's faith and to recruit new members. The fact that it was generally anti-Hitler, anti-war, and pro-religion made little difference to critics of the group. The *Gobitis* decision was handed down in early June 1940, and within days, violence erupted against the sect as they tried to distribute their literature. In Harrison, members who were distributing pamphlets were attacked by a mob shouting "fifth columnists" and were forced to flee the city. Newspapers reported similar attacks against the group throughout the state. The eastern Arkansas cities of Monette and Pocahontas even adopted city ordinances that required "all persons wishing to distribute literature, make public addresses, or preach, to request permission three days in advance." Similar statutes were passed by other cities. Many leading citizens supported these punitive measures. An editorial in the *Sharp County Record,* published in Evening Shade, a neighboring city of Pocahontas, condoned the violence against the sect because "the American people will not allow much public activity by these enemies of America and American institutions. They will have to do their work in the dark, which of course, is exactly in line with their doctrines and practices." To the Witnesses the enemies of the United States were not the Axis powers of Europe but the representatives of those powers in the United States. "To discredit our exposure of their schemes," wrote one member, "Nazi fifth columnists use the fact that we do not salute the flag or 'Heil' men to stir up false patriots among citizens. The Nazi plague has advanced so far in America that freedom of speech and assembly can be shut down anywhere."[6] The mobs that attacked the Witnesses in Arkansas were by no means Nazi sympathizers, but they were guilty of taking patriotism to the extreme.

Not only did mobs and city governments deny the Witnesses religious freedom and the constitutional rights of free speech and assembly, so did some Arkansas courts. In Texarkana, W. M. Manning, a veteran of World War I, a former member of the American Legion, owner of the largest photography shop and supply house in the city, and a highly respected citizen—before he became a Witness—was arrested and convicted on charges of desecrating the flag and distributing un-American literature. During Manning's trial a circular letter in his defense was handed to presiding Judge J. D. Cook from J. Edgar Hoover, director of the Federal Bureau of Investigation. The letter urged FBI agents and federal district attorneys to prevent interference with the Witnesses' rights of free speech and assembly, because FBI investigators had found no connection between the sect and Nazi or other un-American groups. Responding to the letter, Judge Cook said "neither Mr. Hoover nor any United States Attorney is enforcing the law in Arkansas," and he instructed local law enforcement officials "not to lay [sic] down on the job because of the sentiments of some wheelchair artist in Washington." Then, before a packed, applauding courtroom, he gave the defendant the maximum sentence allowed—thirty days in jail and a $100 fine.[7] Despite hostile attitudes faced by Witnesses in Texarkana and other Arkansas cities, they continued to try to practice their faith in the midst of growing mob violence and legal prosecutions.

In June 1942, the Witnesses received another setback when the state supreme court ruled on an appeals case involving Joe Johnson, an unemployed member of the sect from Marshall. In June 1941, Johnson had been arrested and convicted in Marshall for showing public contempt for the flag. He was fined $50 and sentenced to twenty-four hours in jail. Johnson had been arrested after refusing an order from Neil Cooper, a Marshall welfare commissary worker, to salute the flag as a precondition for receiving his monthly welfare food allowance. Cooper testified at Johnson's trial that the Witness not only refused to salute the flag but angrily said that "it doesn't have eyes, it doesn't have ears, it is only a rag." Cooper also claimed that Johnson said he "would rather die before saluting the flag." The court sustained the sentence given the defendant by the Searcy County Circuit Court on the grounds that "calling the flag a rag is a clear expression of contempt."[8] Chief Justice Griffin Smith, lone dissenter in the case, said that the court and Arkansas were no better than its wartime enemies "if we succumb to the ideologies of those who enforce obedience through fear and write loyalty with bayonets."[9]

Arkansans appeared to be oblivious to the 1940 circular letter from the FBI clearing the Witnesses of involvement in un-American activities and to the dissenting opinion of Chief Justice Smith in the Johnson case, because attacks on the sect continued throughout 1940 and 1941, escalating after the Japanese attack on Pearl Harbor. In January 1942, members of the John C. Carroll Post of the Veterans of Foreign Wars in El Dorado attacked members of the sect on the streets while they were attempting to distribute literature. The veterans seized the materials, burned them, and forced the group to flee the city. In Harrison, veterans of the Spanish American War formed the Ozark Mountain Men's Club to combat the Witnesses, because "they circulate un-American literature, encourage disrespect for the flag, and undermine the government."[10] Other extralegal groups also organized elsewhere in the state. By the summer of 1942 it had become clear to the Witnesses that the Four Freedoms—freedom from want, freedom from fear, freedom of speech, and freedom of religion—did not apply to them.

Violence against the Witnesses reached its peak in the fall of 1942 when the sect gathered in Little Rock for its annual convention. Using its official name, The Watchtower Bible and Tract Society, the group applied for and received permission to use Traveler Field, a local baseball park in North Little Rock, as a convention site. They planned to use the arena for a joint assembly during which time they were to hear, by wire transmission from Cleveland, Ohio, a message on peace from N. H. Knorr, their national leader. Before they could gather, however, the M. M. Eberts Post of the local American Legion discovered that the Watchtower Bible and Tract Society were actually Jehovah's Witnesses and persuaded the Traveler management to reverse itself and deny the sect use of the facility. Legionnaires also asked the police to evict the group from the city and, when the police refused, they attacked sect members on the streets.[11] The Witnesses, however, refused to be intimidated and continued to search for a convention site.

After failing on several attempts to secure suitable accommodations, the sect obtained the use of a service station on Asher Avenue and adjacent land operated by J. W. Mercer. It was located near a camp that housed laborers working on Stretch 3 of the War Emergency Pipeline. On the night of September 20, 1942, some of these workers, shouting "fifth columnists," attacked the Witnesses as they prepared for their meeting. Seven members were shot and others beaten with blackjacks and heavy pieces of metal pipe while a crowd of bystanders stood by and cheered. The beatings administered were so severe that one of the spectators turned pale and almost fainted as he watched. When the police arrived, sect members, including the severely wounded, were arrested and charged with disturbing the peace. Authorities said none of the pipeline workers were arrested because they could not be identified. Indications were that local law enforcement officials shared the sentiments of one of their colleagues from Camden, Arkansas, who described the sect as "a well-organized minority who were the vanguards of the fifth column of destruction in America," and declared that they "had to be stopped before they spread farther in the land." [12]

The few Arkansans who were willing to defend the rights of Jehovah's Witnesses also suffered for their attitudes. J. W. Mercer, the service station operator who had consented to let the sect use his facility as a convention site, lost his lease on the property the day after the attack by the pipeline workers. Oscar Winn, a one-armed, sixty-five-year-old Little Rock attorney who agreed to defend imprisoned members of the sect was attacked on the streets of the city and severely beaten as he attempted to gather information for the defense of his clients. Even Witnesses who were not present at the Asher Avenue incident suffered from economic persecution. The local American Legion and other "patriotic" groups, arguing that "any person willing to take good salaries from the state and the defense industries should also be willing to fight for the country and salute the flag," forced private and state employers to fire employees who were Witnesses. Many of those who lost their jobs had been employed by the same firm or state agency for years prior to the war and had good work records. [13] Local draft boards also attempted to force Witnesses, some of whom had been granted CO status prior to 1942, into the armed forces.

Under Section 5-G of the Selective Service Act of 1940, religious dissenters could be exempted from military service as combatants if they agreed to accept noncombat military positions or war-related civilian employment. All applications for CO status had to be approved by the applicant's local draft board. This provision, however, did little to benefit the Witnesses because it was generally applied to those religious groups with a formal doctrine and a clearly defined administrative structure. Since the Witnesses had no formal religious hierarchy or doctrine, they found CO status difficult to obtain. The very nature of their religion required that each member serve as a minister in order to carry the Christian message to the world. They believed that their God-given duty to preach the gospel would be restricted if they served in the military in any capacity; therefore, they sought CO status under class IV-D— Ministerial status. Unlike regular CO status, a IV-D classification exempted one from all forms of military service and civilian war-related duty.[14] Witnesses felt that without a IV-D classification they could not fulfill their earthly ministry.

In Arkansas, after Pearl Harbor, it was quite a task for Witnesses to persuade local draft boards to grant them CO status, especially class IV-D. The local draft boards consisted mostly of middle-class professionals, businessmen, and farmers, and they were formally appointed by the president on the recommendations of the state governor. Arkansas' wartime governor Homer Adkins, a veteran of World War I who had entered politics as a Ku Klux Klansman, had no sympathy for pacifists, especially Witnesses. Most of his recommendations to the president for local draft board service reflected his views. The evidence suggests that the governor and local draft boards shared the sentiments of one of their fellow Arkansans who, shortly after the attack on Pearl Harbor, wrote:

> I stood before the American Legion hut and watched Old Glory wave over it. I tried to imagine a swarm of Japanese hoodlums swarming that hut telling our servicemen to bow to Allah. I tried to imagine Hitler stomping into our churches and telling our pastors you can't do that: My thoughts? How could any American be a conscientious objector?

That was the attitude Witnesses faced in Arkansas when they applied to their local draft boards for a IV-D classification. They were frequently told by their local boards that "you are going to jail or the army, one of the two."[15]

A typical example was that of Albert Hamilton Blakely. Blakely was an ordained Witness minister, a lifelong resident of Geyer Springs, a small community adjacent to Little Rock, and an employee of the Arkansas Highway Department (AHD) between 1934 and 1942. In 1940, he applied for and was granted ministerial status by his local draft board. But after the outbreak of violence against the Witness conventioners in Little Rock, Blakely was fired by AHD and reclassified 1-A as available for immediate military duty. His

AHD supervisor told him that he was dismissed due to strong pressure from the American Legion, and his local board informed him that he was reclassified because of unacceptable public conduct.[16]

Blakely was not immediately drafted, and in June 1943, he requested his local board to restore his classification as a "pioneer" (the Jehovah's Witnesses term for minister), basing his request on a 1942 directive from General Lewis B. Hershey, national director of Selective Service. Hershey had ruled that anyone engaged in more than eighty hours per month of ministerial work could claim IV-D status. To support his appeal, Blakely presented evidence to show that he preached to between 75 and 115 persons every Sunday and Wednesday and performed other ministerial services. The local board ignored the evidence and denied Blakely's appeal. Determined to get a hearing, the frustrated Witness, using his right to appeal local board decisions, wrote the state director of Selective Service, requesting that his case be heard at the higher level. But the state director, who felt that the Witnesses "were lower down than a snake," denied his request. As a final resort Blakely wrote a three-page, single-spaced letter to General Hershey, explaining his case and requesting the restoration of a IV-D classification. In late 1943, Blakely was informed by General Hershey that his case had been taken to President Roosevelt and that his ministerial status had been restored. The whole process had taken three years. It is interesting to note that Blakely's IV-D status was returned in 1943, the year in which inductions into the armed forces reached their peak and in which the United States Supreme Court handed down two decisions that favored the Witnesses.[17]

In March 1943, the Supreme Court ruled that "cities may not prohibit the distribution of handbills merely because the handbills invite the purchase of books for the improved understanding of religion or because the handbills seek in a lawful fashion to promote the raising of funds for religious purposes." Although the case had its origins in Paris, Texas, the ruling applied to Arkansas because several cities in the state had enacted ordinances requiring Witnesses to pay a peddler's tax before the distribution of their literature and to request advanced permission before making public speeches. The Court, also in 1943, reversed its decision in the *Minersville School District v. Gobitis* case and ruled in *West Virginia State Board of Education v. Barnette* that "words uttered under coercion are proof of loyalty to nothing but self-interest." The decision struck down the compulsory flag salute in West Virginia's public schools and changed similar statutes across the nation. The two Supreme Court decisions, combined with General Hershey's directive, restored the right of Witnesses to practice their faith in public and the right of their children to refuse to salute the flag in public schools. Isolated attacks against the sect continued throughout the nation after 1943, but in Arkansas they declined sharply. Public attention now focused on another group of Americans who were hated more than the Witnesses of Jehovah.[18]

The Unwanted: Japanese-Americans in Arkansas

Wartime restrictions placed upon the civil liberties of Jehovah's Witnesses were minor when compared to the indignities suffered by Japanese-Americans during World War II. Unlike the Witnesses, who had taken their positions voluntarily, Japanese-Americans lost their civil liberties because of race. Many believed that Japanese-Americans would have more loyalty to Japan during the war than to the United States. Therefore, the decision was made to remove them from the West Coast to relocation centers in the nation's interior. This forced evacuation of over 100,000 persons was one of the most blatant mass violations of civil liberties in the history of the United States. The decision to relocate was a military one that was sanctioned by the Supreme Court. "In time of war," ruled the Court in the case of Gordon Hirabayashi, a Japanese-American student at the University of Washington who had refused to obey an order to report for relocation, "residents having ethnic affiliations with an invading enemy may be a greater source of danger than those of different ancestry." From the viewpoint of the Court, it was not its duty to question the wisdom of the military officials.[19]

Four days after the attack on Pearl Harbor, the Western Defense Command was established under the direction of General John L. DeWitt. The entire West Coast was declared a theater of war, and as a security measure, Secretary of War Henry L. Stimson, supported by West Coast businessmen and politicians, urged President Franklin D. Roosevelt to remove all Japanese citizens as well as aliens. General DeWitt, however, was opposed to the mass removal of all Japanese because he believed that such a move would alienate those who were loyal. "An American citizen, after all, is an American citizen," he told advocates of removal. Consequently, President Roosevelt, acting on the advice of DeWitt, refused to authorize the relocation of Japanese-Americans.[20]

In January and February 1942, Manila and Singapore fell to Japanese forces, and fears of an enemy invasion of the American mainland engulfed the West Coast. Feelings toward Japanese-Americans were mixed, but support for removal was almost unanimous. Some citizens feared for the safety of loyal Japanese-Americans who might be attacked by irate Americans and supported removal for this reason. Others saw the war and removal as a convenient opportunity to rid themselves of competition from prosperous Japanese-American businessmen. These special interest groups, composed of various California chambers of commerce, the American Legion, the California Joint Immigration Committee, the Native Sons and Daughters of the Golden West, and many others, pressured DeWitt and their congressmen to remove all Japanese. Leading the clamor for removal was California Attorney General Earl Warren. The future chief justice of the Supreme Court believed strongly that the Japanese were a serious security threat. By February 1942, General De-Witt had changed his position and threw his support behind a removal program for all Japanese because, as he expressed it, "A Jap's a Jap and it makes no difference whether he is an American citizen or not. There is no way to determine their loyalty." Thus, because of national security concerns, the desire to profit economically from the misfortunes of Japanese-Americans, and pressure from politicians, the decision was made to move all persons of Japanese ancestry from the West Coast to interior relocation centers.[21]

On February 19, 1942, President Roosevelt, acting on the advice of military authorities, issued Executive Order 9906, authorizing the war department to designate military areas within the United States and to exclude any and all persons from them. The order was utilized only once and only on the West Coast against Japanese-Americans. To administer the removal program, President Roosevelt, on March 18, 1942, issued Executive Order 9102. This order created a civilian agency, the War Relocation Authority (WRA), which was assigned the task of collecting and transporting the designated potential enemies to new "homes" in the nation's interior. The WRA did its job with brutal efficiency. In a hundred and thirty-seven days more than 110,000 persons of Japanese ancestry, two-thirds of them American-born citizens, were forced to sacrifice their homes, businesses, and personal keepsakes and were herded into trains for transport to hastily constructed relocation centers. The evacuees were allowed to take only some clothing, bedding, and utensils. No pets were permitted. Forced to sell their possessions for whatever they could get, the evacuees suffered income and property losses of approximately $350 million. According to Henry Sugimoto and his wife, who were relocated in Arkansas and returned to the state for a visit in 1979, their new "homes" were "bleak, dirty, military in nature, cold and unwelcoming."[22]

Ten camps were established. Two were erected in southeast Arkansas at Jerome in Chicot County, and at Rohwer in Desha County. The 19,505 acres of land chosen for the centers in Arkansas were tax delinquent properties owned by the state. State officials were anxious to return this potentially good farmland to private ownership but lacked the capital and other resources needed to make necessary improvements. Most of the acreage was snake-infested low-land, covered with young timber, and more than one half of it was under water during winter. Yet it was rich Mississippi delta farmland known as "buckshot" soil. The centers at Jerome and Rohwer were to serve not only as wartime housing for relocated Japanese-Americans but also as agricultural colonies. Consequently, the evacuees were required to help clear the land, produce their own fruits and vegetables, part of their own meat supply (each camp raised its own pork), and grow other crops that were needed for the war effort. For those not engaged in agricultural work, small-scale manufacturing jobs were provided. Salaries were as low as $12 to $19 per month, a meager sum compared to what the evacuees had been forced to give up. Work on the camps began in July 1942 and continued through January 1943. The first full contingent of evacuees arrived on September 18, 1942, and the last left November 10, 1945.[23] When the first internees arrived, construction of the Jerome and Rohwer camps was unfinished. Few staff members knew anything about the background of the internees or the aims of the WRA. Time, however, revealed that they were people of integrity and honesty.[24]

The majority of the ten thousand Japanese-Americans relocated in Arkansas were American citizens: Nisei (second generation, American-born) and Sansei (third generation, American-born children of American-born parents). However, they differed greatly in their socioeconomic backgrounds. Those sent to Rohwer were generally from the Santa Anita, California, assembly center. Before internment, according to Edgar V. McCoy, the WRA's community analyst at Rohwer, most "were large-scale farmers and businessmen who exhibited a higher level of advancement and Americanization than the internees at the Jerome center." Those at Jerome came from the Fresno, California, assembly center and were mostly small-scale farmers without much sophistication.[25] Many of the internees in each camp were understandably bitter because they saw themselves as loyal Americans who were being unjustly treated. But the majority of them cooperated with WRA authorities and other camp officials because they felt it would serve as proof of their loyalty.

The fact that the Japanese-Americans relocated in Arkansas were American-born citizens made little difference to the majority of Arkansans who viewed them as an enemy race. Governor Homer Adkins had informed officials long before the first internees arrived that they would not be welcomed. In fact, Adkins told federal authorities, when they first inquired about relocating some of the West Coast evacuees in Arkansas, that "the only way I can visualize where we can use them at all would be to fence them in concentration camps under wire fence and guards."[26] He only agreed to accept the evacuees after the war department requested that he do so as a patriotic duty. Federal authorities also had to promise the governor that they would accept full responsibility for the safety of the evacuees while in Arkansas, keep them under a guard of white troops, and immediately remove them after the war. A number of other Arkansans shared similar sentiments, and there was hostility directed at the evacuees almost as soon as they arrived in the state. They quickly discovered how they were going to be received when local construction workers denied them the use of bathroom facilities built on the camp site.[27] They also discovered that most of the state's services were off limits to them.

When the Japanese-Americans removal program was first announced, officials at the University of California interceded with colleges and universities in the relocation states to accept their students. They compiled and circulated a list of institutions that had responded favorably. The only listed Arkansas institution was the Agricultural and Mechanical College at Monticello (Arkansas A & M). This embarrassed Marvin Bankston, president of the college, who quickly announced that "my school does not want any Japs." He said that Arkansas A & M got on the list through a misunderstanding of his response to the letter of inquiry from California. Bankston explained that he had worded his reply in such a way that California officials "would not think an Arkansas school would simply refuse to consider the question."[28] But in reality, that was his position as well as that of Governor Adkins and other state educational leaders.

A survey of Arkansas college presidents by Ralph B. Jones, state commissioner of education, on the question of accepting relocated Japanese-American students into state institutions, revealed that they were all opposed to the proposal and considered it "an unjustifiable demand in light of the strong racial feelings entertained by citizens of Arkansas and students of the various colleges." Governor Adkins also rejected the proposal, due not only to his strong anti-Japanese sentiments but also because he saw in it an opening through which blacks might seek entrance into the state's all-white educational institutions.[29] Adkins considered both black Americans and Japanese-Americans as being inferior to whites and was unwilling to do anything that might contribute to their upward mobility.

Once the evacuees began arriving in large numbers during the summer of 1942, public reaction was generally unfavorable. Some resented the evacuees because of their racial ties to Japan. Others disliked them because they feared that they would become permanent residents of the state and economic competitors in the postwar period. This view was expressed by a plantation manager near the Rohwer camp who accused the WRA and California businessmen of using Arkansas as a dumping ground for the Sunshine State's economic competitors and undesirables.[30] Similar sentiments were expressed by Reverend J. B. Hunter, a former Methodist missionary to Japan. Hunter charged that "under the guise of war the big fellows who run politics and business in California have called upon the government to get rid of their competition." Those charges were substantiated by Austin Anson, managing secretary of the Grower-Shipper Vegetable Association of Central California, who admitted he and his colleagues were using the war to get rid of their Japanese-American competitors.

Public resentment of the new arrivals was somewhat alleviated by Governor Adkins and the press. The governor told critics of the evacuees that he had been assured by the federal government that the internees would not be allowed to compete with local labor while in the state and that they would be immediately removed after the war. An editorial in the *Arkansas Gazette* told those concerned about a permanent Japanese-American presence in the state to set aside those fears because "the land they will clear and develop seven to fifteen times its value will not be theirs—they will have no claim." Once informed that the evacuees would be removed from the state after the war and that their stay in Arkansas would mean thousands of dollars to the local economy, in addition to the increased value of the swampy property cleared for the camps by the evacuees themselves, residents near the camp areas became more receptive to the establishment of the camps. But some still could not reconcile the idea of having "Japs" in their communities and appealed to the governor and the WRA to change their minds.[31]

Not all Arkansans were opposed to the relocation program. Some saw the establishment of relocation centers in the state as an excellent opportunity for Arkansans to put their professed Christian faith into practice. The Methodists were the most vocal in welcoming the evacuees and encouraging people to extend to them Christian principles. Two hundred ministers at the Arkansas Pastors School at Hendrix College, Conway, adopted a resolution in June 1942 welcoming the newcomers. The "Layman's Page" of the official church publication, *The Arkansas Methodist,* urged readers to "let the Methodists of Arkansas extend to those unfortunate people a hand of Christian greeting and brotherliness. They are the victims of the folly and madness of war. . . . Let it never be said that we were found wanting."[32]

The Methodists were not the only religious sect that attempted to attend to the needs of the evacuees in Arkansas; numerous other churches established branches in the camps, but most were the results of individual rather than organized denominational action. Many of these were of short duration. Even official spokesmen for the Methodists backed away from religious activity in the camps once they were firmly established. In fact, the bishop of the Arkansas Methodist Church told his ministers that "it would be best to stay away from that group in a wire enclosure." Consequently, a number of Methodists who had gone to work in the camps as missionaries quit after a short stay, because "they believed that they were corrupting their young by letting them associate with the evacuees."[33] The call for the extension of Christian principles to the internees was never fully embraced by religious groups in Arkansas. However, the churches did not completely abandon the internees as many of them remained active in the camps for the duration of the war.

One of the more hostile organizations that the WRA and the evacuees encountered was the Arkansas Medical Society (AMS) which demonstrated an early anti-Japanese attitude by refusing to provide medical care. The organization also tried to prevent nonmembers from practicing medicine in the camps. After the first full contingent of Japanese-Americans arrived at the Rohwer facility in September 1942, the AMS made no effort to offer them its services. When it learned that Dr. M. B. Lynch, a Tennessee physician employed by the construction firm that was building the camps, was also treating evacuees, it secured an injunction from Chancellor E. G. Hammock of Desha County prohibiting Lynch from practicing medicine in the camp because he did not have a state license. Hammock's injunction against Lynch, however, was overruled by the state supreme court in November 1942. The court declared that the WRA camps were federal projects and under the "exclusive jurisdiction" of the federal government and outside the realm of Arkansas law. The "exclusive jurisdiction" rule allowed out-of-state doctors and non-AMS members to practice in the camps with the approval of the WRA. But it also gave enemies of the evacuees a weapon to use against them. Responding to an inquiry from state health officer Dr. W. B. Grayson as to whether doctors in the centers could legally issue Arkansas birth certificates to camp newborns, state Attorney General Jack Holt said they could not, ruling that since Arkansas law did not apply to the camps under the "exclusive jurisdiction" rule, "neither a physician with nor one without a license to practice medicine in this state may make a birth certificate within these centers."[34] Since the WRA wanted to operate the camps according to local laws and did not keep records for in-camp births, Holt's ruling had the effect of denying infants born in the relocation centers legal existence, without which they could not qualify for inheritance rights or federal and state benefits, if any became available, after the war.

The WRA was a civilian agency and it never accepted the "exclusive jurisdiction" rule. The agency believed that the centers should be subject to the local laws of the communities and states in which they were located. The WRA, therefore, directed Robert A. Leflar, its regional attorney, to seek a reversal or modification of the "exclusive jurisdiction" rule in Arkansas. Leflar, after discussing the issue with Guy E. Williams, the new state attorney general who had succeeded Holt in 1943, was advised to file a disclaimer petition against the rule with the governor and the state supreme court. The governor and the court accepted the WRA's waiver of "exclusive jurisdiction" and thereafter the relocation centers were subject to Arkansas' health and civil laws.[35] The record, however, does not indicate that the AMS voluntarily offered its services to the evacuees after the repeal of exclusive federal jurisdiction.

In addition to legal problems surrounding the relocation centers, the Arkansas congressional delegation and state authorities were continually bombarded by complaints from residents charging that the state's public schools were being drained of qualified personnel by the higher wages paid to teachers in camps, that the evacuees were receiving more favorable treatment in regard to food rationing than local residents, and that the evacuees wasted supplies and refused to work up to expectations. In Washington, WRA director Dillon S. Meyer met with the Arkansas congressional delegation on October 22, 1942, and answered the charges. He explained that teachers in the camps were paid slightly more than public school teachers because they worked for twelve months compared to nine for public school teachers and because they worked under adverse conditions. And "it was simply not true," he said, "that the evacuees were receiving favorable treatment regarding food rationing." Meyer said food rations at the centers were the equivalent of army B rations, costing only forty-five cents per day.[36] The delegation was also informed that the camps, once firmly established, would grow part of their own food.

The Arkansas congressional delegation, accompanied by reporters from the *Arkansas Gazette* and *The McGehee Times,* toured the Jerome and Rohwer camps in November 1942. They found no evidence to substantiate the charges of favoritism in food rationing or in other services and appeared to be satisfied with Meyer's earlier explanation of camp conditions. Nevertheless, local residents continued to complain about the slow pace of the evacuees in clearing camp lands for cultivation. The complaints were so numerous that E. B. Whitaker, field assistant director of the WRA in Arkansas, felt compelled in January 1943 to remind local critics that "the problem of cutting green wood [in winter] in a buckshot swamp is a Herculean undertaking and you don't expect a person to change overnight from an office worker or a merchant [which

were the backgrounds of the majority of the evacuees at Rohwer] to a woods-
man and a farmer, regardless of his race or color." [37]

By 1943, the relocation centers in Arkansas had their full quota of occupants, many of whom volunteered for work outside the camps in order to help
relieve the tremendous wartime labor shortage from which the state suffered.
Governor Adkins, however, refused the requests. "I don't mind them leaving to
work in other states," he told a group of defense contractors who had inquired
about the possible use of workers from the camps, "but as a matter of policy I
am not going to recommend that Japanese work in any capacity in this state."
In fact, Adkins did not want the evacuees to leave camp grounds unless they
were leaving the state. In January 1943, he assured I. C. Oxner, who had complained that the evacuees were not only being allowed to leave the camp and
shop in McGehee, but were also being allowed to speak their native language,
that he would "pressure the superintendents of each camp to keep the internees on camp grounds and under guard at all times." Following Oxner's
complaint, Adkins filed a written complaint with WRA authorities about the
lax discipline exercised by guards at the relocation centers. The Arkansas internees considered themselves loyal Americans and resented Adkins' attitude,
especially his adamant refusal to allow them to work in the state. One angry
internee at Rohwer told the governor that "when you refuse an American the
right to work in the war effort, thereby hindering production, you are a saboteur, and a saboteur of the worst kind." Adkins' critic, who said that he was a
veteran of World War I, also gave the governor his opinion of Arkansas in
general. "Your empire from every conceivable angle," he wrote, "is one of the
poorest—culturally, economically, socially, and politically. And if it is your
fear that we might get involved in your messy social systems, then banish that
fear, for we are too intelligent, too well educated, and too 'Americanized' to
have any part of it." [38] Although the internees tried to keep a low profile in
Arkansas and avoid involvement in what many of them saw as an antiquated
socioeconomic system, fate would not allow that to be.

The provincialism of wartime Arkansas was clearly revealed in November
1942 when Private Louis Furushiro, a uniformed Japanese-American soldier
stationed at Camp Robinson near Little Rock, was shot and seriously wounded
in a Dermott cafe while en route to visit relatives incarcerated at the Rohwer
camp. His assailant was a local farmer, W. M. Woods, who had two sons in the
armed forces. Woods entered the eatery, saw Furushiro, and asked: "Are you a
Jap?" When the soldier replied in the affirmative, Woods opened fire.

A few days later another violent incident involving the evacuees occurred
outside the Rohwer camp when C. M. Brown, a local farmer who was return-

ing home from a deer hunt, wounded with buckshot two evacuees who were outside the camp on a work detail. Brown said that he thought the evacuees, with the help of their white supervisor, were trying to escape. After making a "civilian arrest," he marched his captives two and one-half miles to McGehee and turned them over to local police. To his surprise, the prisoners were released and Brown was arrested and charged with assault and intent to kill. Although some local citizens let WRA officials know that they did not condone violent acts against the evacuees, there was little sentiment for bringing Woods and Brown to trial. In fact, the circuit judge and the local prosecuting attorney tried to persuade WRA officials to drop all charges against them. Local authorities felt it would create more ill will toward the evacuees if the defendants were brought to trial and that it would be a waste of time and money, because a jury of their peers would not convict them for their crimes. When the WRA refused to drop the charges, local officials, over the objection of the agency, reduced the charges against the defendants from assault with intent to kill to the lesser charge of assault with a deadly weapon. The defendants pleaded guilty to the reduced charge and were freed after paying the minimum fines.[39] Although there were no more reported cases of physical violence against the internees, the state press continued to attack their loyalty, and there were more efforts to enact harsher restrictions.

Leading the parade of Arkansans who wanted more severe measures was Governor Adkins. In December 1942, Adkins, preparing for the January 1943 opening of the legislature, wrote the secretary of state for California requesting information about a California law which denied certain minorities the right of property ownership in that state. "It is my understanding," wrote Adkins, "you have a statute in California that prevents certain races, including Japanese, from owning land in your state. I would appreciate having a copy of this statute and if there are charges I will be glad to send a check for same." [40] The governor wanted the information so that the legislature could pass a similar measure during its 1943 session. He wanted to make sure that Japanese-American residents of Rohwer and Jerome would have no reason for wanting to remain in Arkansas after the war. Apparently he got what he wanted from California, because when the 1943 legislature convened, several bills designed to prevent the evacuees from becoming property owners in Arkansas were introduced.

Of all the discriminatory legislation introduced in the 1943 legislature, only Senate Bill No. 11 was enacted into law. That statute, sponsored by Senator B. Frank Williams of Osceola, a representative of the state's large planters, prohibited any person of Japanese ancestry or birth from owning land in Arkansas. Williams charged that the law was necessary "on account of the low standard of living of the Japanese people." Due to their low living standards, according to Williams, "a white person cannot profitably compete with the Japanese in agriculture or business." The Osceola legislature told his colleagues that his bill "guaranteed that no Japs can stay in this state." Both branches of the legislature shared Williams' views, and his bill passed the Senate by a vote of 30 to 0. In the House the vote was 76 to 1. Governor Adkins signed the bill into law on February 13, 1943.[41] Another bill introduced by Senator Richard K. Mason of Camden would have barred all members of the Mongolian race from attending white public schools in Arkansas. It passed the Senate by a large margin, but it failed to get a majority of votes in the House and was never enacted into law. Although there were enough votes in the House to prevent passage of the Mason Bill, the majority of legislators were still strongly opposed to the education of Japanese-Americans. They registered their displeasure through the unanimous adoption of a resolution which protested the policy of the WRA that allowed evacuees to leave Arkansas to attend colleges in other states. The resolution accused the WRA of practicing favoritism, since loyal American youth in the armed forces were denied the opportunity to pursue a higher education.[42]

The humiliation suffered by Japanese-Americans in the relocation centers in Arkansas, as they read about the actions of the 1943 legislature, appeared to be of little concern to anyone but themselves. The bitterness and bewilderment felt by the evacuees manifested itself in numerous ways inside the barbed-wire compounds that they were forced to call home. The mandatory communal style of living—community dining halls, toilets, and shower facilities—not only destroyed morale, but also led to a breakdown in the manners of children and the traditional strong unity of the Japanese family. Juvenile delinquency among young boys and promiscuity among girls became major problems, and those youths who did not become social problems existed in a world of confusion and bitterness. Some were able to leave Arkansas and find civilian employment in other states where they were well received. One who left the Rohwer camp with his family and settled in Kalamazoo, Michigan, wrote back to his camp teacher: "Out here the kids make me forget that my nationality is Japanese and they have initiated me into two clubs."[43] Most, however, were not so fortunate.

Nothing revealed more clearly the bitterness and confusion of the youthful internees than a series of essays written for a tenth grade English class at the Jerome center in January 1943. One student from Los Angeles, California, wrote: "The last three years of my junior high school education were the best of my life, with the exception of the last couple of months. These were the disconsolate months. 'Remember the Maine,' the battle cry of the Spanish-American War changed to 'Remember Pearl Harbor' . . . we were relocated here in Arkansas. My future is something still in a fog and cannot yet be determined." [44] Another used his essay to attack the federal government and the WRA. The embittered student wrote:

> Many of us feel that the mass evacuation of the Japanese, both citizens and non-citizens, in the name of military necessity was not a just and adequate way to handle the situation.
>
> They, the first generation, without the least knowledge of the English language nor the new surroundings, came to this land with the pioneer spirit of settling. They worked hard to give their children the necessities of the American way of life . . . only to have it shattered by the order of evacuation. [45]

Just as the hopes, aspirations, and dreams of the first generation of Japanese were destroyed by Executive Orders 9066 and 9102, so too were those of their descendants—Nisei and Sansei—who were American-born citizens.

To many Arkansans, the inhabitants of camps Jerome and Rohwer represented the World War II enemy; few acknowledged the fact that the internees were American citizens who had sacrificed sons in defense of the United States and American democracy. A Jerome inmate, writing near the end of the war, expressed the bitterness:

> Add to all of the feelings that you, the public have and include the loss of everything that was personal to you; being in these segregation centers for over three years; giving your sons for the cause of democracy, of which these mothers don't quite fully realize the meaning; being segregated and now more or less forced out again without the financial situation that you, in the normal state of living have been able to accumulate during the boom years. The mothers here can't even give an atmosphere of home to these sons who have been away for so long. You mothers know how your sons appreciate you and home. [46]

Although the inmates of camps Jerome and Rohwer were denied most of the pleasures and privileges that a normal home life provided, they made the best of a difficult situation. They did their jobs without complaint and were, in general, cooperative with WRA officials. Things were so peaceful among the more sophisticated internees at Rohwer that "Rohwerites often remarked, jokingly, that they wished they could have one good riot, one paralyzing strike, and even a murder or two," while the internees at Jerome developed "a curious sort of civic pride in their wartime homes." When the government decided to close the facility in 1944, they vigorously protested. The Jeromians wanted the WRA to close the Rohwer facility instead because they felt it was inferior to their own. They were especially disturbed when rumors spread that their camp was to be converted into a German prisoner-of-war facility. Jerome residents felt that they were "actual if not technical prisoners of war and had as much right to their camp as the Germans." To register their discontent and to request that Jerome be kept open, they appealed directly to Secretary of Interior Harold Ickes, arguing that their center should be maintained because of its good appearance, its improved drainage system, the good morale of the residents, the beginning of an extensive agricultural program, and the importance of the camp to Nisei soldiers stationed nearby at Camp Robinson, outside of Little Rock. Whereas the more Americanized residents of the Rohwer facility were anxious to leave their camp, the occupants of Jerome were not.[47] Evidently, the Jeromians had discovered a certain amount of security during their internment.

The desires of the occupants of Jerome had little impact on governmental wartime decisions. On June 30, 1944, the camp was closed, and shortly thereafter it was turned into a German prisoner-of-war facility. The 2,750 Japanese-American internees who were still in the camp—thousands had left the camps in Arkansas for wartime jobs in other locations—were sent to the Rohwer facility and to relocation centers in different states. On December 17, 1944, the war department announced the revocation of Executive Order 9066 to become effective November 30, 1945. After that date evacuees were free to return "home." The physical nightmare was over, but horrible memories had been implanted in the minds of the evacuees forever. The Japanese-Americans in Arkansas, like the former black slaves in post-Civil War America, could not claim any of the fruits of the backbreaking labor they had rendered in order to make the swamp lands that comprised their camps productive agricultural soil. The land the internees had cleared and developed seven to fifteen times its prewar value was declared surplus property by the WRA, and was later sold by the Surplus War Property Administration at public auction to local farmers for $5 to $10 per acre.[48]

As expected and desired by the majority of local residents, few of the Jerome and Rohwer evacuees chose to remain in Arkansas after their release. The internees, especially those at Rohwer, had never liked Arkansas weather, and Arkansans themselves were held in certain contempt. Some, however, chose to remain in the state and take their chances. The most noted among the few who decided to stay was a group of six families led by Yokochi Nakagawa. Prior to the war and his internment at Rohwer, Nakagawa had been president of the Vineyard Corporation of California. The sudden evacuation from the West Coast had cost him $100,000 but he had been able to retain several of his California farms. After his release he sold one of the farms for $41,000 and purchased 117 acres in the Badget community east of Little Rock where he and his followers settled in 1945. Although anti-Japanese feelings were still running high, the people of the small community showed no resentment toward their new neighbors.[49] Perhaps a small segment of the Arkansas population had come to realize that Japanese-Americans were also loyal American citizens, and it was time to get on with the business of granting equal opportunity to all Americans.

5 Black Arkansans: The Quest for Home Front Democracy

> We will keep our record of faith and trust in the American people and in our God who has led us, as of old, into this good day of privilege and opportunity to serve our country and humanity.*

America's entry into World War II found black Americans outside the nation's social mainstream. They existed and functioned on the peripheral edge of society where they experienced few of its political and socioeconomic opportunities.[1] This was especially true in Arkansas where the great bulk of the black population was comprised of tenant farmers and poverty-stricken sharecroppers and where Jim Crow laws were strenuously enforced. Many black Arkansans had believed that their service in the armed forces during World War I—that great crusade to make the world safe for democracy—would open the doors of opportunity for them at home. That did not happen. However, they saw World War II as another chance to serve the nation and win acceptance by whites, which in turn would open to them the avenues of opportunity.

Whereas many blacks in the nation were willing to wait for the post-World War II period before aggressively pushing for equality at home, others desired immediate action. They feared that justice delayed would be justice denied. Black leaders across the nation realized that if progress was to be made in postwar America, the groundwork had to be laid during the conflict. Black leaders in Arkansas shared those views. Beginning with the inauguration of the national defense program in 1940, black Arkansans began to push for an equal share of the benefits of American democracy. Their wartime goals were equal employment opportunities, protection for the civil rights of black civil-

---

*Resolution adopted by the Arkansas Negro Chamber of Commerce, Little Rock, shortly after the United States entered World War II. *Arkansas Gazette,* December 14, 1941.

ians and black soldiers stationed in Arkansas, equal pay for black employees of the state, and a representative voice in state politics.

The Battle for Equal Employment Opportunities

Black Arkansans experienced little of the economic benefits generated by the defense program that began in 1940. Although large numbers of blacks were unemployed and eagerly sought jobs, they found it difficult to secure employment in the defense industries. When they complained, they were told that they did not have the required skills. In March 1940, at the Little Rock, Arkansas, Interracial Conference on the Employment Problems of Negroes, Laurence Oxley of Washington, D.C., supervisor of the Negro placement service of the bureau of employment security, told blacks that they needed more training in the fields of competition in order to increase their efficiency and employment opportunities. Black leaders were cognizant of that fact, but they also knew that white political and business leaders in Arkansas were unwilling to provide the economic and physical resources needed for blacks to improve their competitive positions. The last thing that the white supremacist leaders of the state wanted was a class of well educated and well trained competitive blacks. This position was clearly expressed by Eli W. Collins, director of unemployment compensation of the state Department of Labor. Collins told the conference that what a black Arkansan needed "was not training in the fields of competition, but in those areas in which he is traditionally accepted—domestic, custodial, and agricultural work." [2] Collins realized that if blacks were trained for skilled jobs, the state's large agricultural and business interests—which employed the majority of blacks—would lose their supply of cheap labor.

Following the Interracial Conference on the Employment Problems of Negroes, Dr. W. H. Metzler, a University of Arkansas sociologist, urged state officials to improve economic opportunities for blacks in order to preserve domestic peace. Metzler argued that the state had to take action because "Negroes were migrating to the cities where they were being employed at the lower occupational levels and were becoming frustrated and receptive to the rhetoric of un-American radicals who promised them higher wages, opportunity to become farm owners, unemployment insurance, and other benefits they are unable to deliver." The un-American radicals to whom Metzler made reference were union organizers and agents for the Farm Security Administration (FSA).

Unions, especially the Congress of Industrial Organizations (CIO), which

wanted to organize industrial and agricultural workers, had increased their organizational activity in Arkansas coincidental with the escalation of the national defense program. The FSA, a New Deal reform agency, was also operating several programs that were designed to convert tenant farmers and
sharecroppers into small independent operators in the state. In Arkansas, the
CIO and the FSA were considered to be Communist conspiracies against the
liberties of free people. To preserve democracy, Metzler wanted the state to
make concessions to blacks in order to keep them from supporting such
groups. Metzler was no liberal; he was a typical conservative Arkansan who
believed that minor concessions to blacks would result in their continued loyalty and support. In that paternalistic attitude that white Arkansans took toward blacks, Metzler said, "the Negro is by nature happy and contented and
will respond to thoughtful treatment." [3] "Thoughtful treatment" for blacks,
however, was not on the agenda of Arkansas business and political leaders.

The desire to limit the employment opportunities of blacks to the traditional
domestic and agricultural jobs was clearly revealed through the administration
of national defense training programs in the state. Although the programs
were federally sponsored and financed, they were controlled by state officials
who were not inclined toward improving the skills of blacks. The programs
began in the summer of 1940, but it was not until year's end that the first program for blacks was begun. In December 1940, a national defense program in
carpentry was started for blacks at the Scipio A. Jones High School in North
Little Rock, the local black school. The class at Jones High was the first one
for blacks and was limited to those with experience in carpentry and a "tenth
grade" education. This requirement severely limited the number who could
qualify for the program because few blacks in rural agricultural Arkansas in
1940 had a tenth grade education or its equivalent. In fact, according to E. L.
Compree, selective service director for the state, the average white male who
was drafted for military service in 1941 did not have the equivalence of a
fourth grade education, and white males, generally, were better educated than
blacks. Skilled labor was in demand by the defense industries in Arkansas,
but the educational requirement for national defense training programs in the
state meant that the majority of blacks would be unable to qualify for those
higher-salaried jobs.

Realizing that Arkansas officials were going to do little to get blacks involved in the national defense program, black leaders appealed to the federal
government for help. An editorial in the *Arkansas State Press,* the state's only
black owned and operated commercial newspaper, called upon federal authorities to "place Negroes as guards of munition factories, shipyards, air-

plane works and give them arms and make them responsible for the safety and security of works and property because our national defense is more important than unreasonable and reactionary racial antagonisms." Not only did black Arkansans complain about their exclusion from well-paying national defense jobs, so did blacks throughout the nation. Nationally those complaints led to a slight increase in the employment of blacks by defense industries in northern and western states. Rumors even spread that the United States Employment Service (USES) was planning to use blacks in supervisory positions in its offices. To the die-hard white supremacists of Arkansas, however, it was tantamount to treason to even suggest that blacks serve as supervisors over white employees. Congressman W. F. Norrell of Fort Smith, reacting to the rumor concerning USES, clearly expressed the position of the majority of the white population in an angry letter of protest to Federal Security Administrator Paul V. McNutt:

> It matters not how great the financial needs of white men and women and how much their need for employment, Southern people in their indignation, will never bring themselves to permit such an outrage as to allow white men, women and girls to be interviewed and supervised by Negroes.

Responding to Norrell's letter, which was frequently quoted by the state's white newspapers, the black editor of the *State Press,* Lucious Christopher Bates, curtly quoted Voltaire: "Prejudice is the Reason of Fools."[4] Prejudice may have been the reason of fools, but in Arkansas it was deeply rooted in customs, traditions, and was legalized by Jim Crow statutes.

Despite the protest of blacks against job discrimination by the defense industries throughout the nation, the Roosevelt administration was intransigent when it came to increasing significantly their employment opportunities. This was especially true for the southern part of the nation. To Roosevelt, the votes of conservative southern Democrats for his legislative programs took precedence over the civil rights of black Americans. Although the majority of blacks who could vote supported the reelection of the president in 1940, he had never publicly championed civil equality. Even if the president agreed with the demands of black Americans, it was not politically feasible for him to do so openly, and Roosevelt rarely committed himself to any cause that did not hold a political advantage for him. The president's position changed only after black civil rights activist and labor leader A. Philip Randolph, president of the Brotherhood of Sleeping Car Porters Union, threatened a massive march on Washington to protest the exclusion of blacks from the defense boom. Randolph planned to march down the Washington Mall on July 1,

1941, with some 50,000 to 100,000 blacks so that the world could see how American speeches in defense of democracy and social justice were hollow mockeries. Such a march would not only have embarrassed the administration, it would have also served as an excellent propaganda tool for American Communists—who had actively sought black support—and for the Axis powers of Europe. Initially, Roosevelt dismissed Randolph's threat but quickly realized that he and his black supporters were serious. Therefore, the president, through the intervention of his wife Eleanor, promised black leaders that he would use his authority to end job discrimination in exchange for a cancellation of the protest march.[5]

On June 25, 1941, President Roosevelt, after issuing a statement deploring racism, issued Executive Order 8802 which forbade discrimination in federal job training programs and in private industries that accepted government contracts. The decree also established a five-man Fair Employment Practice Commission (FEPC) to ensure enforcement. The establishment of the FEPC appeared to be a major achievement for blacks, but in practice it proved to be less than effective. It was, in fact, a paper tiger, because it could not fine or reduce the profits of industries that ignored Executive Order 8802.[6] The order was a political coup for Roosevelt and a major hoax for black America. The president and business leaders knew that Congress and the public would not allow production to be halted by cries of racial discrimination. All was not lost, however, because some employers in northern and western states, without being forced to do so by the government, increased their employment of blacks, but in the South, especially in Arkansas, the usual pattern of stringent Jim Crowism continued unabated.

In late 1942 employment opportunities for blacks in the defense industries in Arkansas and the South began to improve. Improvement, however, was not due to the effectiveness of continued black protest, nor to a dramatic change in the views of southern whites; rather it was due to development of a serious labor shortage caused by the demands of the armed forces for manpower. The domestic labor shortage was so severe by October 1942 that Ed McDonald, regional director of the War Manpower Commission for Arkansas, Missouri, and Oklahoma, directed the managers of war industries in his region to "use women and minority groups previously denied employment and to begin now—not tomorrow."[7] With the greater employment of blacks in Arkansas and the South facilitated, black leaders in Arkansas turned their attention to other immediate wartime problems.

The Black Soldier and the Battle Against Jim Crow

During World War II the army, for disciplinary and other un-explained reasons, sent southern recruits north for basic training and reversed the process for northern inductees. This created problems for black soldiers from northern states who often ran afoul of Jim Crow laws and traditions. Southern whites were determined to make sure that northern black troops adhered to these laws and traditions regardless of how humiliating they may have been. This often resulted in serious and sometimes violent confrontations between northern black soldiers, white civilians, and law enforcement officials in the South.

The first clash between northern black troops and white Arkansans took place in southwest Arkansas near the small town of Gurdon. According to a report filed with Governor Homer Adkins by State Police Commissioner William C. Yarbrough, the incident occurred when a state patrolman stopped the singing and marching all-black 94th Engineers Battalion from Fort Custer, Michigan, on a state highway and ordered their white officer to keep the black troops quiet when in the presence of whites. The patrolman wanted the black troops to observe the southern tradition that required groups of blacks to keep silent in public when in the presence of whites as a sign of respect for their superiors. When the white officer of the 94th Battalion refused the trooper's order and told him that "Negroes were as good if not better than white people," he committed a serious violation of southern tradition. The state patrolman was so angered by the officer's comment that he physically attacked him, an attack that brought the black soldiers to their officer's defense. According to Yarbrough's report and newspaper accounts, local white witnesses to the incident began screaming riot and sent to Little Rock for guns and ammunition after all supplies had been exhausted in Gurdon, and prepared to make war on the black soldiers. A violent confrontation was avoided when additional state police arrived, and in conjunction with other white officers of the 94th Battalion, order was restored. The incident was a foreshadowing of what awaited black troops sent to Arkansas for basic training.[8]

Following the Gurdon affair there was almost constant friction between black soldiers and white civilians and police who were determined to make the soldiers realize that their uniforms did not mean that they had achieved racial equality. That friction resulted in the shooting death of Sergeant Thomas B. Foster on the streets of Little Rock in March 1942. Foster was a member of the all-black 92nd Engineers Battalion, stationed at Camp Robinson. During an alleged riot on Little Rock's Ninth Street—a black business and residential area—Foster was shot five times by city policeman A. J. Hay. The chief of police and county coroner, C. C. Reedy, conducted an investigation of the shooting and ruled it justifiable homicide. The ruling was made after Hay testified that he shot Foster after he and his partner, George Henson, had gone to the assistance of military police (MP) who were being harassed by a hostile crowd of blacks led by Foster while the MP's were trying to arrest another black soldier on an intoxication charge. Hay said that he only fired after the soldier knocked him to the ground and charged him with a club. The investigators accepted Hay's account of the incident without questioning any black witnesses who called the shooting a cold-blooded murder. As far as city officials were concerned, the report of the county coroner and the chief of police closed the case. But the attitudes of black Arkansans had changed, and they were unwilling to let what they considered an obvious case of murder pass without protest.[9]

The Foster shooting left Little Rock's black community seething in anger. Many black Arkansans shared the sentiments of black columnist George Schuyler of the *Pittsburgh Courier* who said in December 1940 that "Our war is not against Hitler in Europe, but against Hitlers in America." A black soldier who witnessed the Foster shooting cried openly. He threw his neatly pressed cap to the ground and asked: "Why should we go over there and fight, these are the sons-of-bitches we should be fighting." His words were directed at no one in particular but they represented every white person who had called him "Nigger"—all the suppressed emotions of a lifetime of racial oppression.[10] The city's only black newspaper described the Foster shooting as "one of the most bestial murders in the annals of Little Rock tragedies," and an independent investigation of the "murder" by a group of black citizens organized as the Negro Citizens Committee of Little Rock (NCCLR) concluded that: 1) Foster was prostrate on the ground and unarmed when shot, 2) the MP's did not give the soldier proper protection, and 3) the large crowd of black spectators made no attempt to interfere with the MP's but under the influence of mass psychology attempted to push close to the center of excitement to see what was taking place. Based on NCCLR's reference to the crowd and mass psychology, Sergeant Foster had apparently questioned the tactics used by the MP's while arresting his fellow soldier for drunkenness. It was that act that led to the intervention of city police and Foster's death. In Arkansas, no black military or civilian person had the right to question the tactics used by white police while arresting a black, regardless of the harshness used. By doing so, Foster had directly challenged white supremacy and had to pay the ultimate price so that others would not entertain such ideas. Copies of

NCCLR's conclusion, along with a call for a federal investigation of the Foster shooting, were sent to President Roosevelt, to the attorney general of the United States, to the commanding officer of Camp Robinson, and to city officials. Little Rock had no black policemen when Foster was shot; consequently, NCCLR called upon the city to hire black policemen to patrol those areas of the city frequented by black soldiers and to give them the authority to arrest any violators of the law regardless of color. NCCLR concluded its report to city officials by declaring that "the Negro does not want to be free from the white man, he wants to be free with him." [11]

In June 1942, Attorney General Francis Biddle, responding to NCCLR's request and to similar complaints from blacks throughout the nation, ordered a federal investigation of the Foster incident. On June 11, the United States grand jury for the eastern Arkansas division convened to begin deliberations on the case. Blacks—who had always looked to the federal government for justice—believed that the jury would indict city policeman A. J. Hay for murder, but the presiding Judge T. C. Trimble, a native Arkansan, virtually directed the jury to dismiss the case. He admonished the jury "to use common sense" and not to return an indictment if it "would not serve some useful purpose." To the predominantly white jury—three blacks had been selected for purposes of appearance—the implication of Trimble's charge was clear: the indictment of a white policeman for the murder of a black while making an arrest would serve no useful purpose in Arkansas. Based on prevailing white racial attitudes, which condoned the use of violence against blacks as a means of social control, the indictment of Hay would have not only led to a decline in law and order but also in a more aggressive attitude by blacks in defense of their civil rights. After a short period of deliberation, the jury decided not to indict the policeman and reported to the judge that "the shooting of Sergeant Thomas B. Foster has been investigated, considered, and ignored." [12] Justice for blacks in Arkansas had been rendered.

Leaders of Little Rock's black community immediately criticized the grand jury's report and increased their calls for the hiring of black police. Reverend Emanuel C. Dyer, pastor of Little Rock's First Baptist Church and an NCCLR member, urged Camp Robinson officials to request the army not to send soldiers to the city "if they are black in skin." Another NCCLR member, Reverend G. Wayman Blakely, pastor of the Bethel A.M.E. Church, asked whether the government was training men to fight the Axis "or to be shot down with the least provocation, if indeed any provocation, like rats in the streets. Let us have Negro policemen on West Ninth Street," he urged city officials, "and until this is done, place on West Ninth Street the most experienced and level-headed men who are not Negro haters." The black-owned *State Press* launched an editorial crusade against police insensitivity toward black soldiers and blacks in general. The attacks were so relentless that Little Rock's downtown merchants, who felt that the paper's fiery editorials were costing them business and giving the city a bad name, attempted to force the paper out of business by withholding advertising from it. When that failed, the editor, L. C. Bates, was offered a bribe—the return of advertising revenue—to mute his criticism of police and city officials. Bates refused and told his would-be bribers that the paper "was published for the defense of Negroes of Arkansas and the benefit of the publisher." [13]

Black criticism of Little Rock city officials and the local police brought the city's white press to their defense. An editorial in the *Arkansas Gazette* accused black leaders of making "unjustified and scurrilous" attacks on local authorities. The conservative *Arkansas Democrat,* in a "Run of the News" article, charged that Sergeant Foster's death was not the result of police brutality or insensitivity to black civil rights but the result of "a nationwide campaign by the black press and the National Association for the Advancement of Colored People (NAACP) to use the war to undermine white supremacy on the home front." [14] The *Democrat's* article struck at the core of the issue—the maintenance of white supremacy in Arkansas and the South. The *Democrat* conveniently chose to ignore the concluding statement of NCCLR'S report on the Foster shooting which had declared that "the Negro does not want to be free from the white men, he wants to be free with him." [15]

Following the Foster case, the 92nd Engineers Battalion, to which he had belonged, was transferred to another area, but military and government officials had become more aware of the problems faced by black troops in the South. Due to that awareness, federal authorities in 1942 began to prosecute southern police officers for the killing of black soldiers on the grounds that the soldiers' civil rights were being violated. Following the arrest of two white policemen in Texas for shooting a black soldier who was charged with violating the Lone Star state's Jim Crow laws, the *State Press* credited military officials, not local law enforcement agencies, for the arrest, because military "big wigs have realized that if Japan and Germany are to be conquered, the South must be conquered first." The paper hoped that authorities in Arkansas, in view of the Texas case, would realize that they could not continue to violate the rights of black soldiers with impunity. The comments of the *State Press* were timed to coincide with the arrival, in August 1942, of the next detachment of black troops that was sent to Camp Robinson for training. Military officials were aware of the Arkansas situation, and when the troops arrived, their commanding officer, Major Richard Donovan, in a speech to the Little Rock Lions Club, requested that they urge local police "to make less use of the nightstick technique of reasoning with black soldiers." He also encouraged city officials to hire black policemen to patrol those areas patronized by his men.[16]

In August 1942, the Little Rock City Council, reacting to pressure from the black community, Camp Robinson officials, and the local business community, hired the city's first black policemen to patrol West Ninth Street. However, they were limited to that neighborhood and to other black areas of the city and could not arrest whites without the assistance of white policemen. Eight black patrolmen were hired over the vigorous objection of the Little Rock Policemen's Association (LRPA) which argued that the lawless element of the black community would not tolerate being arrested by their own race and that to assign a black to the tough Ninth Street area would be equivalent to signing his death warrant. What the LRPA did not realize or chose to overlook was the fact that black policemen, more often than not, were just as tough, or tougher, when dealing with their own race as were white police. The objection of the LRPA to the hiring of black patrolmen was not based on a genuine concern for their safety; rather it was based on the desire to keep the city's police force all white, and it consistently worked to make the tenure of the black policemen on the force unpleasant. In June 1943, the LRPA was able to persuade the city council's police committee to insert into the contracts of black officers a clause which required them to waive all pension benefits.[17] The obvious attempt to force the black policemen to resign failed; they remained on the job despite LRPA's opposition and the decision of the city council's police committee. Although Little Rock's black policemen were not given the same arrest authority as whites and were denied the pension benefits enjoyed by their white counterparts, the fact that they were on the force served to reduce tension between blacks and white police in the city.

Equal Jobs, Equal Pay: Black Public School Educators in Pursuit of Equality

Public schools for black Arkansans were much inferior to those for whites in terms of facilities and teaching materials provided by either the state or the local school boards. The salaries of black teachers correlated with the facilities in which they worked. Many black teachers used part of their meager wages to purchase teaching materials for their classrooms in an attempt to provide students with an equal education, but there was little they could do to persuade the state and local school boards to equalize salaries. Black teachers throughout the nation faced the same problem and some of them, believing that salary discrimination was illegal, took their case to the federal courts. In 1940, the Supreme Court ruled, in *Alston v. School Board of the City of Norfolk* (Virginia), that wage differentials between white and black teachers were discriminatory and violated the due process clause of the Fourteenth Amendment. Although the ruling applied to public schools throughout the nation, it was not adhered to in Arkansas. In a 1941 report published by the Urban League, low salaries were identified as the principal handicaps confronting black teachers in the state. Records of the state Department of Education showed that the average salary for the state's 10,574 white teachers in 1941–1942 was $625 compared to $367 for blacks. In March 1941, black teachers in Little Rock petitioned the local school board for salary equalization. The board referred the request to the state Department of Education where the state commissioner of education, Ralph B. Jones, urged black educators to "be reasonable because changes must be gradual." Jones estimated that it would cost Arkansas $1 million to initiate a program of equalization.[18] Nothing was done.

In March 1942, Scipio A. Jones, a local black lawyer acting on behalf of Susie Morris and the black Classroom Teachers Association (CTA) of Little Rock, filed a salary equalization suit in the United States District Court against the Little Rock School Board and the superintendent of schools, Russell T. Scobee. The suit charged that the Little Rock School Board had violated the Fourteenth Amendment rights of black teachers by refusing to pay them salaries equal to those of whites. Reaction by white education officials to the CTA's suit was predictable. Commissioner Jones denounced it as "untimely and ill advised" and accused the CTA of trying to take advantage of the national crisis (WWII) "to accelerate advantages which are already far ahead of the vast majority of situations elsewhere."[19] In the federal court of Judge T. C. Trimble, the Little Rock School Board claimed that the Fourteenth Amendment rights of black teachers had not been denied. School board lawyers argued, in words filled with cleverly concealed charges of black inferiority, that black teachers were paid less than white teachers because "Negro teachers differ as compared to whites in degrees of special training, ability, character, experience, duties, services, and accomplishments." Judge Trimble, after hearing arguments from both sides, refused to rule on the issue of racial discrimination and dismissed the CTA's suit on the grounds that the organization was an unincorporated body and as such could not sue or be sued in federal court. However, Trimble did agree to a motion by the plaintiff's lawyers to try the salary discrimination charge of Susie Morris on its own merits.[20]

During the separate Morris trial, the plaintiff was represented by local black lawyers Scipio A. Jones and J. R. Booker. Assisting them was Thurgood Marshall of New York who represented the NAACP. Basing their case on the Fourteenth Amendment's due process clause and the Supreme Court's decision in the 1940 *Alston* case, the lawyers argued that their client was the victim of racial discrimination because white teachers with lesser qualifications were paid more. They noted that 22.3 percent of the state's white teachers had less than one year of college training and argued that Morris was better qualified than many of her white counterparts and should receive at least equal pay because she had earned a B.A. degree from Talladega College in Alabama, grades of "A" in graduate English courses from the University of Chicago, and had seven years of teaching experience. John L. Lewis, Morris' principal at Dunbar High School, testified that she was an excellent teacher and that he had recommended to Charles R. Hamilton, the white principal of the Garland school who made the final evaluation, that she receive an "A" rating. Lawyers for the school board and Superintendent of Schools Russell T. Scobee admitted that black and white teachers had to meet the same qualifications to receive identical teaching certificates but argued that Morris was paid less than white teachers because she only rated between three and four on the five-point rating scale. Scobee also testified that he accepted Hamilton's ranking of Morris in determining her salary because he was more experienced and reliable than her principal. The defense also argued that teacher salaries were not based solely on educational achievements but also on cultural background, personality, cooperative spirit, and additional intangibles that black teachers could not satisfy. The intangibles were the beliefs of white administrators that blacks were racially and culturally inferior and that no amount of education could make them equal to whites. This was revealed in the testimony of school board witness Annie Griffey, a white supervisor of primary teachers in Little Rock with thirty-one years of experience. Griffey testified that white teachers were paid more than blacks because "regardless of college degrees and teaching experience no white teacher in Little Rock is inferior to the best Negro teacher."[21] Based on the testimony of the defense, it was clear that black teachers were paid less than their white counterparts because of their alleged racial inferiority.

In January 1944, Judge Trimble handed down his decision in the suit. He chose to ignore the Supreme Court's decision in the *Alston* case and ruled that "the issue of racial discrimination is not deemed essential to a final disposition of this case. The Court is of the opinion," he said, "that the defendants have the right to fix the salary of each individual teacher according to their [sic] real worth and value to the system as teachers, and are not required to set up and adhere to some arbitrary standard of college degree, years of experience, or some other mechanical method of determining salaries." In short, Trimble decided to support the continuation of white supremacy in Arkansas by ruling that race was not an issue in the Morris case. The decision, declared the *Arkansas Democrat,* "rests on the bed-rock principle of the American system." Lawyers for the plaintiff immediately appealed, and in June 1945 the United States Court of Appeals at St. Louis reversed Trimble's ruling and ordered the Little Rock School Board to equalize the salaries of white and black teachers.[22] It was only fitting that black Arkansans should win a victory over home front racism in the summer of 1945 because the nation's armed forces—which included thousands of blacks—had just defeated Nazi Germany and its philosophy of Aryan racial supremacy. The victory, however, was a minor one, because the major and most controversial battle in wartime Arkansas for home front equality was in its most crucial stage.

One Man, One Vote: Black Arkansans and the Quest for Political Democracy

In March 1942, a black high school student in Fort Smith, Arkansas, was invited to speak to the local Rotary Club on the desires of blacks in war and peace. The youth told his all-white audience that "the Negro is willing to give his life for this country the same as whites but in return the Negro feels he should have a voice in governmental affairs." The response of the all-white audience to the student's statement was one of dead silence, for they knew that it would take a major restructuring of state politics before blacks would be able to express an effective voice in state government. The Democratic Party of Arkansas (DPA), which controlled state politics, used various methods to minimize the political role of blacks in the state. The two most effective devices were the "all-white" Democratic primary and the poll tax. Under the rules of the DPA only qualified white electors could become party members and cast votes in its primary elections. Because there was no strong Republican opposition, whoever won the Democratic primaries was almost guaranteed victory in the November general elections. Thus, the primary vote was more important than the general election ballot. Blacks who held a poll tax receipt—most did not because the majority were sharecroppers and rarely saw cash money before World War II—could vote in the general elections, but the races had already been won in the primaries. Since the state only recognized those candidates endorsed by the DPA as the official Democratic candidates for public office, blacks were automatically denied a role in selecting and electing those persons who directly influenced their daily lives.[23] The right to cast ballots in the Democratic primaries was the main political goal for blacks during the time of the Second World War.

Prior to the 1920s, few blacks in Arkansas considered themselves Democrats and made no real effort to join the DPA which they had historically viewed as the party of slavery. But politically astute blacks saw that affiliation with the DPA was the only way that they would be able to influence their destiny in the state. In 1928, inspired by the Supreme Court's decision in *Nixon v. Herndon* (1925) which outlawed a Texas statute that prohibited blacks from voting in that state's Democratic primaries because it violated the equal protection clause of the Fourteenth Amendment, and impressed by the campaign of Alfred E. Smith, the Democratic nominee for president, black Arkansans, led by Dr. J. M. Robinson, a Little Rock physician, sought affiliation with the DPA. Organized as the Arkansas Negro Democratic Association (ANDA), Robinson and his followers believed that the *Nixon v. Herndon* decision had given them the right to vote in primaries and they petitioned the DPA for the ballot. There was no response from DPA officials. However, when members of ANDA appeared at the polls to cast their ballots they were turned away. Robinson then, with the support of the Little Rock chapter of the NAACP, filed suit against local officials of the DPA on the grounds that the rights of blacks guaranteed by the Fourteenth Amendment had been violated.[24]

The case of *Robinson v. Holman* was argued before the Arkansas Supreme Court on March 17, 1930. The court dismissed ANDA's suit on the grounds that its Fourteenth Amendment rights had not been violated, ruling that the DPA was not a government entity but a private organization with the right to prescribe qualifications for its members. Lawyers for ANDA immediately filed an appeal motion to the United States Supreme Court, but it refused to review the ruling and the case was dismissed. After 1930, blacks continued to seek the vote in DPA primaries, but few cast votes in the meaningless general elections.[25]

Many white Arkansans mistakenly believed that the low turnout among black voters for general elections was due to the repressive poll tax requirement rather than the closed Democratic party. Some opponents of the poll tax viewed the outbreak of war in Europe in 1939 as an excellent opportunity for Arkansas to reaffirm its commitment to democracy by repealing the hated tax.

The voices of dissent, however, were not representative of the state's white majority, as state political and business leaders seized every opportunity to defend the levy. An editorial in the *Arkansas Gazette,* which ignored the penalizing effect of the poll tax on both poor blacks and whites, argued that the tax was necessary because it helped support the state's public schools and kept politics relatively free of corruption.[26] The message of the *Gazette's* editorial was clear—the repeal of the poll tax would open the franchise to the mass of black and poor white voters and force politicians to be responsive to their socioeconomic interests.

Although they detested the poll tax, black political leaders believed that the record employment generated by the national defense program and World War II had made it possible for anyone to pay the tax. Therefore, their primary goal was not poll tax repeal but securing the ballot in the Democratic primaries. They understood the truth of a pro-poll tax editorial published in the *Southwest American* of Fort Smith, which said that "the thing that reduces the Negro's vote in Southern elections is the rule of the dominant Democratic party [in which] none but white voters are eligible for party membership and for a vote in the primaries."[27] The restrictive impact of the all-white Democratic primary was obscured by the issue of poll tax repeal. Although black leaders wanted the poll tax repealed, they were more interested in voting in Democratic primaries, but black leaders were unable to shift the attention of white anti-poll taxers to that issue.

Supporters of the poll tax in Arkansas—the majority of the state's white population—believed that its repeal would lead to the end of white supremacy in the state and to the social equality of the races. Black leaders were quick to point out to pro-poll taxers that their goals were not social but political equality. The editor of the *State Press* summed up the views of the black community on the issue when he wrote:

> If the compound word "social equality" was restricted from the English language, there would be many white people who would be lost for something to hide behind when it comes to granting the Negro his constitutional rights. There are white people who know they can get the support of their people against any movement that would elevate the Negro from his restricted state in life if they even mention the word "social equality."
>
> If social equality meant equal association of the races, and such a plague did exist, we would be willing to stake our anticipated freedom resulting from a victory over the Jap-Nazi powers, that those who are always ranting and mostly

concerned about social equality would get mighty damn lonesome if they depended on Negro association.[28]

Other blacks tried to assure pro-poll taxers in a less virulent tone that all blacks wanted was political equality through the free exercise of the ballot in Democratic primaries. Repeal of the poll tax, however, continued to be the chief topic of discussion.

In 1943, an anti-poll tax bill reached the floor of the United States House of Representatives for debate. Arkansas congressmen joined other southerners in vigorous opposition to the measure. The position of the Arkansas delegation was revealed in late 1942 when one of the constituents of Congressman Oren Harris wrote to suggest that the abolition of the tax would bring national unity and aid the war effort. In his reply Harris said national unity was not an issue in the poll tax controversy and asked: "How in the name of high heaven can the abolishment of the poll tax aid the war effort in any way?" Congressman Harris saw no connection between the struggle of minorities in Europe against Nazi racism and the struggle of blacks at home for equality, and he was not alone in his views. During the House debate over the poll tax bill Congressman Brooks Hays from Arkansas' Fifth Congressional District told Congress that the bill "is an immoral thing" and urged his colleagues to defeat it because it was "cruel and unusual punishment for the South." However, it was Congressman Ezekiel C. Gathings of West Memphis, who represented Arkansas' First Congressional District, who most clearly explained the South's opposition to poll tax repeal. Gathings told his constituents that he voted against the bill because "we cannot have white supremacy in Arkansas and at the same time support a federal act which abrogates state election laws."[29] Despite the strong southern opposition to the anti-poll tax bill in the House, it passed and was sent to the Senate for final action.

During the Senate debate, Arkansas' black Democrats, represented by Dr. J. M. Robinson, the president of ANDA, tried once again to focus attention on the all-white Democratic primary and away from the poll tax. In a letter to the state's senior senator Hattie Caraway, Robinson described the poll tax bill as "the great boogaboo bill" and said that "the passage of this bill *per se* without some form of amendment will do very little good . . ." He suggested that Caraway lead or support a move to amend the bill that would in effect outlaw the white primary. There was no response from the senator, and the anti-poll tax bill never came to a vote due to a southern filibuster, but Caraway undoubtedly would have voted against it. This was indicated by the senator when a reporter asked her opinion of the measure and she snapped in reply: "I am from the South. Do I have to say anything else?" [30]

Although Congress had temporarily removed the poll tax as a national political issue, it indirectly became a topic in Arkansas politics in 1943. The controversy developed when state senator W. H. Abington (White County), as a patriotic gesture toward veterans and the state's aged, sponsored a bill in the legislature to allow all veterans of World Wars I and II and people over 65 to vote in the state primaries and general elections without paying the required poll tax. The proposed statute, Senate Bill 138, drew the immediate opposition of legislators who saw it as an opening through which blacks might seek to vote in the Democratic primaries and even run for public office. "This bill," charged Senator Joe Sheppard of Russellville, "is trying to change the entire rules of the Democratic party." Sheppard was not concerned about the possibility of blacks voting and holding office in his district but believed that his colleagues needed to be aware of what could happen in their areas if the Abington proposal became law. "There are not many Negroes in my county and it wouldn't hurt me," he said, "but it would be very serious in the districts of some members, who under this bill might find themselves faced with Negro candidates for public office." After Sheppard had pointed out the potential threat that Senate Bill 138 posed to white political supremacy in the state, it was defeated 23 to 7.[31] The defeat of the Abington Bill and the failure to pass a national anti-poll tax bill that same year seemed to have killed the poll tax issue. However, in the summer of 1943 President Roosevelt reintroduced the subject as he sought ways to increase the vote for the Democratic party in the upcoming 1944 elections.

Nationally, the Democratic party had suffered significant losses during the congressional elections of 1942. Republicans gained forty-four seats in the House of Representatives and seven in the Senate. When the new Congress convened in January 1943, it was controlled by a coalition of Republicans and conservative Democrats who were hostile to the administration. Concerned about the Democratic losses in 1942 and his reelection bid in 1944, Roosevelt began to look for ways to improve the Democratic performance in the next national election. The president and his advisors believed that the earlier setback was due to the large numbers of Democrats who were prohibited from voting because they had been in the armed forces or were transient war workers who had failed to meet local residential suffrage requirements. There were approximately ten million servicemen—most of them Democrats, the administration believed—who did not vote in 1942, and the president thought that if the ballot could be given to these men, victory would be assured in 1944. To get ballots to men in uniform, the administration proposed that absentee ballots be mailed to them in advance of federal elections.[32]

The administration's proposal was introduced into Congress in the fall of 1943 as the Green-Lucas Bill but quickly became known as the Soldier Vote Bill. It greatly simplified the process of absentee voting: rather than requiring each soldier to apply for a ballot from his home district, waiting to receive it, and executing it weeks later, all servicemen would receive ballots in advance of federal elections and could mark them at the appropriate time. To supervise the procedure, the bill contemplated a four-man bipartisan War Ballot Commission. In the event of an impasse, a fifth vote would be cast by a Supreme Court justice. President Roosevelt, who had never actively supported black civil rights or poll tax repeal, realized that the Soldier Vote Bill presented a challenge to southern election laws because it bypassed the poll tax and gave all soldiers access to Democratic primary elections. The president was willing, however, to risk southern hostility if it meant more votes for himself and the Democratic party during the 1944 elections. Furthermore, the administration believed that it was on sound legal grounds. According to Samuel Rosenman, one of the president's advisors, "the ballot could be gotten to soldiers only through a bill such as the Green-Lucas Bill which asserts federal supremacy over state law and state constitutions, based upon the war powers of Congress."[33]

The Soldier Vote Bill provided a rallying point for "states righters," "white supremacists," and other critics of the Roosevelt administration in Congress and throughout the nation. Few Arkansans believed the bill was a legitimate attempt to get the ballot to servicemen; rather, they argued that it was another effort to undermine white supremacy in the South. An editorial in the *Southwest American* of Fort Smith declared that "it is another attempt by a bunch of longhaired, starry-eyed meddlers who are using the war emergency to further their own pet ideas of social and political reform." Another Arkansas critic of the measure sarcastically suggested in a letter to the editor of the *Arkansas Gazette* that if the president wanted soldiers to vote he could do it by "letting Mrs. Roosevelt deliver the ballots in person." Eleanor Roosevelt was not very popular in the South because of her liberal association with blacks. But it was Congressman Gathings who once again expressed the real reason why southerners opposed the Soldier Vote Bill when he repeated his argument against the federal anti-poll tax bill. "We cannot have white supremacy in Arkansas," he said, "and at the same time acquiesce in support of the federal act which would unconstitutionally abrogate state election laws."[34] Based on letters to the editors of Arkansas newspapers, editorials, and speeches by Arkansas political leaders on the Soldier Vote Bill, it was quite evident that white Arkansans were not willing to support any measure that could lead to the political elevation of blacks.

Southerners were not opposed to granting white servicemen the ballot, but they were opposed to the administration's bill because they believed it was a clear violation of "states rights" and if passed would establish a dangerous precedent for the future. They did not want to enact a federal law that black veterans could use as leverage to gain the vote in Democratic primary elections after the war. A group of southern Democratic senators, led by John L. McClellan of Arkansas, James Eastland of Mississippi, and Kenneth McKellar of Tennessee, proposed a "state control" bill as a substitute for the administration's Soldier Vote Bill. The "state control" bill merely recommended that the states pass laws that would enable soldiers to cast absentee ballots. This system, which allowed the states to maintain control of the election machinery, also gave them the opportunity to identify black soldiers who requested absentee ballots and to discriminate against them by invoking the rule that forbade blacks to vote in southern Democratic primary elections. The "state control" bill left the all-white Democratic party in the South secure. White political supremacy in the United States would be preserved while the nation fought a bloody world war abroad in defense of racial and political equality. President Roosevelt was not pleased with the "state control" bill which he bitterly described as a "fraud" and a "fool bill," but when it passed the Congress he let it become law without his signature.[35] A bill that gave white soldiers access to the ballot before the 1944 elections was better than no bill at all.

While black Arkansans were interested in the congressional debates about the poll tax and soldier voting, they were more concerned with their own struggle to gain the ballot in the state's Democratic primaries. In 1940, the Arkansas Negro Democratic Association (ANDA) had filed a second petition with the DPA requesting that it modify its rules to permit blacks to vote in primary elections. In an attempt to elicit a favorable response from the DPA to its request, ANDA's president said that "we are not seeking approval for the mass voting of Negroes, only for those who may qualify under challenge." The organization did not explain what it meant by "under challenge," but the reference was to those blacks who had tried to affiliate with the DPA in the past and were not identified with the Republican opposition. Whatever the case may have been, the DPA did not respond to the petition. When the DPA failed to act on its request for the ballot, the organization requested United States Attorney General Francis Biddle to force the DPA to grant qualified blacks the ballot for the 1942 primary elections.[36] The appeal was based upon the guarantee of the Fifteenth Amendment.

Unfortunately for ANDA and its members, 1942 was a bad year for the Roosevelt administration. It was an election year, and the administration was being severely criticized in the South for issuing Executive Order 8802, which had created the FEPC. President Roosevelt was also being criticized for his pro-labor policy and for the lack of positive news on the battlefront. Furthermore, the president did not care enough about civil rights to chance losing southern support for his party or to risk civil strife in wartime. For those reasons Roosevelt and Attorney General Biddle took no action on ANDA's request for aid. With or without federal assistance ANDA was determined to try to vote in the 1942 Democratic primaries. Preparations for the election had begun in 1941 as black leaders urged their people to take advantage of war-generated incomes and pay their poll taxes so they could not be denied the ballot for failure to show a poll tax receipt. An editorial in the *State Press* urged blacks to pay the tax because "A Voteless People Is a Hopeless People." The paper, which generally represented the views of the ANDA, also tried to use the fight for democracy abroad to persuade DPA officials to grant that great privilege to blacks at home. In an editorial supporting ANDA's request for the Democratic primary ballot, the paper asked, "What's wrong with Democracy? There is no question mark about who is to fight for democracy, why should it be one on who is to vote for democracy?" Answering its own question, the paper said that "any man who is good enough to fight for a country that still uses the ballot, the least he can expect is to use the ballot." [37]

By the summer of 1942, ANDA had organized black voters in Little Rock, Pine Bluff, Forrest City, and several other Arkansas cities with large black populations in anticipation of the summer primaries. On the day before the elections, Dr. Robinson, ANDA's president, reminded blacks who were gathered for a political rally in Little Rock to carry their poll tax receipts to the polls and vote "only for those candidates running for national office." Hoping to avoid a confrontation with DPA officials, he told the crowd that if they were denied the ballot to "bow politely and leave the voting booth with little ado." Since the DPA had not officially denied ANDA's 1940 petition for the primary ballot, and because the organization believed it had the constitutional right to vote for federal candidates, an overly optimistic Robinson told the crowd that "I don't anticipate any denials." But to the consternation of Robinson and other black leaders, when blacks went to the polls they were greeted by DPA officials who carried large signs upon which were printed in bold capital letters, WHITE DEMOCRATS ONLY.[38] Rebuffed in 1942, ANDA quietly began to organize for another try in 1944.

While ANDA was treating the wounds suffered in 1942 and gathering its forces for another assault on the "all-white" Democratic primary in 1944, the United States Supreme Court moved to spare it what would have been, in all probability, another defeat. On April 3, 1944, the Court, perhaps more willing than the president and Congress to protect black voting rights, outlawed the all-white Democratic primary. The case, *Smith v. Allwright,* began in Texas when Dr. Lonnie E. Smith, a black dentist from Houston, was denied the Democratic primary ballot by S. E. Allwright, a Democratic election judge in his precinct. The Supreme Court ruled that the Democratic party in Texas was not a private political organization as it claimed, but rather it was an essential part of the electoral process. By excluding blacks from participation in primaries, the state was in violation of constitutional guarantees of the Fifth Amendment. "The great privilege of choosing his rulers," said the majority in an 8 to 1 decision, "may not be denied a man by the state because of his color." [39] The decision effectively outlawed the white primary throughout the South.

Reaction to the *Smith v. Allwright* decision in Arkansas followed the "color line." Blacks were elated. The president of ANDA calmly said that it represented "a long-awaited victory for black Democrats in Arkansas," while the editor of the *State Press* in a fiery editorial commented:

> Since the voting issue has been forced and the Supreme Court has spoken, TAXATION WITHOUT REPRESENTATION will no longer be advocated, or at least practiced in Arkansas any more than Arkansas will stand to see her black "citizens" called to foreign shores to shed blood for Arkansas' freedom and deny them the right to share freedom at home.[40]

While black Arkansans greeted the *Smith v. Allwright* decision with enthusiasm, whites reacted with anger and fear. Practically all of the state's political leaders denounced the Court's action. "The Democratic party in Arkansas is a white man's party and will always be a white man's party," declared Governor Homer Adkins.[41] Congressman Oren Harris of Fort Smith denounced the decision "as a move to stir up sectional strife and racial controversy." Congressman E. C. Gathings of West Memphis said, "this decision threatens to revolutionize the existing social setup and bring back a recurrence of the Reconstruction days of the South." Congressman J. William Fulbright, campaigning for the United States Senate when the decision was handed down, told a cheering crowd in Forrest City that he was saddened by the Court's decision because "I am not for Negro participation in our primary elections, and I don't approve of social equality." Fearing the election of blacks to offices in the heavily black populated counties of eastern Arkansas, Attorney General Jack Holt told a conference of state attorney generals in Memphis, Tennessee, that the decision had to be repealed or modified because "we want no Negro county sheriffs in Arkansas." [42] The long-range implications of the *Smith v. Allwright* decision were clear, and DPA officials moved quickly to develop measures that would preserve white political supremacy in the state.

When the decision was first announced, J. C. Barrett, chairman of the state Democratic committee, said that he believed the ruling nullified Rule 11 of the DPA that limited membership to white Democrats and suggested that election officials allow blacks who held poll tax receipts to vote in the 1944 summer primaries. Barrett also appointed a committee of lawyers to study the full impact of *Smith v. Allwright* on the DPA. The lawyers reported to the state Democratic committee June 4, 1944, and said that the decision did indeed apply to Arkansas politics but could be avoided by challenging the loyalty of black Democrats at the polls due to their past participation in state Republican party politics. The committee suggested changing party rules so that blacks could join but made membership requirements so difficult that few would apply. No action on the lawyers' recommendation was taken by the state committee because Governor Adkins was adamantly opposed to black participation in the Democratic primaries in any form. [43]

The "all-white" Democratic primary was outlawed in April 1944, only two months before the Arkansas preferential and runoff primaries. To deny blacks the vote in those elections, the DPA was forced to act quickly. In early July, Adkins reversed his earlier position and endorsed the suggestion of the lawyers' committee that party rules be changed to allow more flexibility for discrimination against black voters. The change of position by the governor, however, was not indicative of a change of heart or views. In a letter to the state committee chairman, J. C. Barrett, Adkins said that "it is my opinion that these Negroes are not Democrats and never will be Democrats and I want to reaffirm my stand that I think we ought to keep the Democratic party in Arkansas and the South a white man's party, and if necessary, to change the rules in order for the judges and clerks to have the authority that this be done." [44] The governor changed his position from total exclusion of blacks from Democratic primaries to one of limited participation, because he had decided to run for the United States Senate rather than for a third term of office, and he was probably concerned about the possibility of federal prosecution of DPA officials if they denied blacks the primary ballot and the effects of federal action on his Senate bid. This change of position by Adkins came too late for the DPA to develop effective legal challenges. In July 1944 blacks, for the first time in Arkansas history, cast votes in the state's Democratic primary elections. All who went to the polls were allowed to vote after presenting a poll tax receipt and promising to support the Democratic nominees in the November elections. One of the first to appear at the polls in Little Rock was J. H. McConico, the secretary of ANDA.[45] Blacks also voted in the August runoff primary and in the November general elections, but their long-awaited victory was short-lived because the DPA was in the process of amending its rules to make it more difficult for blacks to vote in future primary elections.

In September 1944, the DPA met and devised what the *Arkansas Gazette* called "a very practical solution to the Negro problem." Rule #2 of the party, that limited membership and the primary ballot to qualified white electors was amended to read: "The Democratic party of Arkansas shall consist only of legally qualified white electors, but membership in the party shall not be a qualification for voting in Democratic primaries." Rule #3 of the party, that set qualifications for party members, was amended to require nonmembers, as a prerequisite for the ballot, to agree to support the principles and laws of Arkansas as outlined in the state's 1874 constitution, especially the laws relating to the segregation of the races in public schools, public conveyances, and other lawfully designated places, the laws prohibiting the intermarriage of persons of white and African descent, and the constitutional requirement of the payment of a poll tax as a qualification for voting. The amended rules allowed blacks to vote for candidates for national office and met the requirements of *Smith v. Allwright,* but blacks were still denied the all-important role of helping select party candidates because only party members could nominate persons for the Democratic ticket. The rule changes also eliminated the possibility of blacks running for public office as Democrats because only party members could run for office with DPA endorsement. Under amended Rule #3, blacks who wanted to vote in Democratic primaries as nonparty members would have been forced to accept segregation and discrimination in exchange for a hollow vote. But the amended rules, according to the *Arkansas Gazette,* "were politically sound, logical, and fair." "They were based," said the paper, "on the practical advisability of keeping two distinct races apart in their social relations to the mutual advantage and benefit of both."[46] The *Gazette* was obviously speaking for the state's white supremacists because the changes were designed to humiliate blacks and, in accordance with the wishes of Governor Adkins, to "keep the Democratic party in Arkansas a white man's party."

Although it was not in session when the Supreme Court handed down its decision in *Smith v. Allwright,* when the Arkansas legislature convened in January 1945, it immediately began work to legalize the changes in DPA rules. To achieve that goal, two bills drafted by DPA lawyers and the state attorney general's office were introduced. The bill sponsored by Senator John I. Moore of Helena (Phillips County, in eastern Arkansas) called for the establishment of separate primaries, preferential and runoff, for the election held on behalf of candidates seeking federal office. The Moore Bill completely eliminated blacks from participation in state Democratic politics at the all-important primary level. The second bill, sponsored by Senator L. Weems Trussell of Fordyce (Cleveland County), gave every organized political party in Arkansas the right to prescribe qualifications for its members and for those who desired to participate in Democratic primary elections. The Trussell Bill endorsed the previous changes made in Rules #2 and #3 by the DPA in the fall of 1944. With little debate, both the Moore and Trussell bills passed the Senate without dissent. In the House, the Moore and Trussell bills were sponsored by Representative Jim Linder of Helena (Phillips County) who told his House colleagues that passage of the legislation was essential because of the large black population in eastern Arkansas.[47] The majority of the House membership agreed with Linder since the Moore and the Trussell bills passed, 80 to 2 and 82 to 1 respectively. Ben Laney, elected governor of Arkansas in November 1944, signed the measures into law on February 27, 1945.[48]

The actions of the 1945 legislature established a four-primary system—or double primary, as it was called in Arkansas. Five costly elections had to be held in order to nullify the black vote. There would be Democratic preferential and runoff primaries in which only whites could vote. There would also be two Democratic primaries for federal offices in which blacks could vote but at separate polls. Then, there would be the November general election. All elections were to be held at county expense. The result was chaos. County officials found it difficult to get enough black and white volunteers to serve as judges, clerks, and poll watchers at their respective voting stations, and the counties also complained about the expense of the double primary system. Commenting on the system, the editor of the *Marked Tree Tribune* said that "if Negroes are interested in laughing at white people, there is a fine opportunity currently available."[49]

For black Arkansans, their exclusion from the political process in their state was no laughing matter, nor was it for some whites who supported political equality for blacks. While the double primary law was being debated in the legislature, the Federation for Flat Glass Workers, Congress of Industrial Organizations (CIO), Fort Smith chapter, sent a telegram to the solons to protest the proposal. The telegram described the double primary bill as "a disruptive booby trap in the suffrage path" and denounced it as being "at odds with democratic principles which the nation fights to preserve." The editor of the *State Press* added: "We know this is not within the keeping of the U.S. Supreme Court's mandate. But when it comes to giving the Negro a chance to exercise his rights, the South doesn't give a damn about the Constitution or anything else." In a somewhat less bitter tone the black Arkansas Baptist Convention, at its annual meeting in November 1945, adopted a resolution which called upon the legislature to repeal the double primary law because "it is in direct opposition to those fundamental principles for which our great national government, in our recent World War, gave both her blood and wealth freely without respect for race, color, or creed for democracy and this law reflects discreditably upon the whole of our American citizenry." [50]

The political advantages acquired by white Arkansans as the result of the changes in the rules of the DPA and the actions of the 1945 legislature were quite significant. Not only did they keep the DPA all-white, they also completely excluded blacks from state Democratic politics. The changes also placed the state's national congressional delegation beyond any political pressure that black voters might have applied. Although blacks who were willing to suffer the humiliation required by the amended rules of the DPA could vote in some party primaries, they still could not become party members or nominate candidates for public office. That function remained the prerogative of white party members. Consequently, politicians at the federal level felt little need to represent the interests of their black constituents. Yet, in spite of the restrictions placed on potential black voters, whites still felt insecure.

The 1944 *Smith v. Allwright* decision did not outlaw the poll tax as a voting requirement in state or federal elections. Many whites felt that the tax was the last remaining bulwark against the erosion of white supremacy in the state, and they were concerned that Congress would succeed where it had failed in 1943 and pass a federal anti-poll tax bill. On the heels of *Smith v. Allwright*, rumors that Congress would pass such a law brought angry letters of protest from Arkansans. In a letter to Representative J. William Fulbright—who became Senator Fulbright in 1945—Mrs. Mary B. Saladino of Washington, D.C., who identified herself as a former resident of Fayetteville, Arkansas, the senator's hometown, urged the congressman to vote against any poll tax

repeal measure. "I understand that Senator Bilbo of Mississippi intends to filibuster the anti-poll tax bill when it is introduced before Congress," wrote
Mrs. Saladino, and "I sincerely hope that you will do everything within your
power to support his colleagues in the House." According to Saladino, "the
establishment of a colony for Negroes in Africa would be a wonderful development." Few intelligent white Arkansans desired to send blacks back to Africa as a solution to racial problems, but they did want to continue the pattern
of segregation and inequality in the postwar years. This view was clearly expressed by an Arkansas soldier stationed in Austria during the war. "Since I
have been overseas," he wrote to Senator Fulbright, "I have been appalled by
the racial equality which the army is forcing upon the soldiers. It is impos-
sible to keep the races apart, so the army says. The abolition of the poll tax is
simply another step in the same direction and I urge you to vote against it."
Fulbright shared the sentiments of the soldier, for in his reply he said: "I am
following this legislation closely and am inclined to agree with your views." [51]
The senator was consistent in his position, for at no time during his tenure in
the House and Senate did he support poll tax repeal.

The Supreme Court issued its ruling in *Smith v. Allwright* in the spring of
1944. The counter tactics of the DPA began immediately thereafter, resulting
in the changing of party rules in late 1944 and the establishment of the double
primary system in 1945. Those two developments, combined with the
continuation of the poll tax, left black Arkansans politically emasculated.
Through the action of the DPA and the Arkansas legislature during the war
years, it became painfully clear to blacks that their quest for political equality
was just beginning and that the journey would be a long and difficult one.

6 Agriculture, Industry, and Labor in Wartime Arkansas

Although the Second World War had not been wanted it brought an economic bonanza to depression America. It brought new life to the nation's factories, farms, and businesses, and renewed the economic vitality of the nation's citizenry. Unemployment, the scourge of the 1930s, came to an end. The war, with its demands for soldiers and industrial workers, drained off a farm population that was too large in 1940 and created a shortage of labor for small private businesses as people flocked to the well-paying jobs in the war industries. This was especially true for predominantly agricultural Arkansas, but problems were also created as the wartime demand for agricultural products combined with a declining labor force accelerated the trend toward mechanized large-scale commercial farming. This led to a battle, in Arkansas and the South, between the large agricultural interests, who favored agricommercialization, and small farmers who wanted to maintain the tradition of the independent family farmer. From the viewpoint of larger interests, family farmers had become obsolete and unproductive.

The war also brought new industries to Arkansas, which greatly increased nonagricultural jobs and diversified the state's economy. Following these, however, labor unions attempted to secure for the working man a greater share of the economic pie. This also caused problems because unions, especially the CIO, threatened to organize not only industrial laborers but also tenant farmers and sharecroppers as well. Union organization of the latter group would have automatically placed pressure on the state's large planters to pay their employees higher wages; and Arkansas employers were not known for paying equitable wages to their employees. Unions were not only resented for their efforts to organize workers, increase wages, and improve working conditions, but they were also disliked because large segments of the population looked upon labor's basic weapon, the strike, as traitorous during wartime. Arkansas businessmen during World War II, conscious of the widespread anti-union sentiment among the general public, made a deliberate attempt to permanently weaken and discredit unions.

The Battle of the Farmers: The Arkansas Farm Bureau vs. the Family Farmer

One of the more prosperous groups in the Unites States during World War II was the farmers. Despite the dwindling agricultural labor supply, farmers were asked to produce more with less, and they did. They were able to meet the challenge through the increased use of machinery and longer work days. The heightened productivity of farmers was reflected in rising incomes. Nationally, farm income by 1945 had increased 250 percent. But in the midst of growing farm prosperity, small farmers were gradually being forced out of business. Between 1940 and 1945, the number of farms in Arkansas decreased by 4.7 percent. The decline was due to a number of factors: the abandoning of small unprofitable farms for jobs in the war industries, the natural trend toward agricultural commercialization, and a desire on the part of some large operators to eliminate their small competitors.[1]

Representing the large agricultural interests both nationally and in Arkansas was the Farm Bureau. This agency had almost collapsed during the depression but had been saved by the New Deal's Agricultural Adjustment Administration (AAA). Its members were the chief beneficiaries of the AAA programs, and the Farm Bureau became a wealthy and powerful organization. It was able to take advantage of the demands for agricultural products generated by World War II to propel itself into the position of spokesman for the nation's large farmers. The wealth of these interests had developed partly from AAA payments that large farmers received to take land out of production to reduce agricultural surpluses and stabilize prices during the depression. According to AAA regulations, landowners were supposed to share their AAA payments with their tenants and sharecroppers in order to prevent disruption and additional unemployment, but most did not. Instead, they evicted them and kept the payments for their own use. Moreover, once they were on their feet again, they used their power to attack other New Deal programs that were designed to benefit small family farmers and those tenant farmers and sharecroppers who had been uprooted by the AAA program. The goal of the bureau was complete control of American agricultural production.[2]

The interests of small farmers and displaced tenant farmers and sharecroppers were represented by the Farm Security Administration (FSA), which was created in 1937 by the Bankhead-Jones Farm Tenancy Act. It was the first federal agency to do anything substantial for the tenant farmer, the sharecropper, and the migrant worker. The FSA had its origins in the New Deal's Resettlement Agency which had been directed by the social planner and reformer Rexford C. Tugwell, the undersecretary of agriculture during the mid-1930s. The FSA administered two basic programs for displaced tenant farmers and sharecroppers: (1) collective farming—a process through which the agency purchased abandoned arable land for settlement, and (2) a loan program through which tenant farmers and sharecroppers, who could not get loans elsewhere, could obtain long-term low interest loans to purchase small farms. It also administered several social programs for the rural poor. Thus, the FSA catered to the poorest of the rural poor who were mostly southern and white. About one-fourth of FSA clients were blacks who mirrored the conditions of their white counterparts. This group usually provided the backbreaking labor for the state's large agricultural enterprises, but the FSA, to the dismay of the Farm Bureau, began gradually turning these people into successful small farmers.[3]

In 1941 there were 23,981 FSA borrowers in Arkansas. Most of these were small landowners and former tenant farmers and sharecroppers and, reported Hudson Wren, FSA director for Arkansas, they were hardworking, honest, and conscientious people. According to Wren, they had become FSA clients in the summer of 1940 and by the end of the fiscal year in June 1941, they had increased their annual incomes from an average of $396 to $596 per year. To FSA clients the agency was the symbol of the New Deal for farmers, not the AAA. In 1942, the FSA began to expand its lending program for small farmers and rural families in order to increase the production of foodstuffs for the wartime Food for Freedom Program. The expansion of the program in Arkansas drew additional hundreds of poor and marginal farmers under the FSA umbrella because of the opportunity to become property owners and to make a profit from the wartime demand for agricultural products. It was the FSA's attempt to increase food production and the income of its clients that brought the Farm Bureau's smoldering resentment of the agency in Arkansas out into the open. The state's basic agricultural crops—cotton, vegetables, and fruits—were labor intensive. They required a large supply of seasonal labor that was cheap, and it was this labor supply that the FSA was converting into small successful independent farmers. Big farmers were not pleased with what they called "subsistence agriculture" and sought ways to eliminate the competition. The general non-farm public was unaware of the fight taking place between the Farm Bureau and FSA clients; they only saw rising food prices.[4]

There were three programs considered by the government to increase wartime food production. The first, favored by the Farm Bureau, proposed to increase the price of all farm products. The second, supported by the AAA, called for the payment of cash bonuses to farmers for the production of certain staple crops. The third, supported by the FSA, which represented more than 3,000,000 small farmers nationwide, called for increased production and distribution of farm products and an increase in agricultural aid for small farmers. In the final analysis, the government decided to encourage farmers to produce more and let the laws of supply and demand, with some modifications, dictate prices. Subsequently, the FSA, which for some time had boasted of its role in the national defense effort, increased its aid to small farmers. This expansion of FSA programs threatened to limit the profits of the large farmers by reducing their pool of cheap labor. The Farm Bureau had never liked the social programs of the FSA, and under the cover of the wartime economy it launched a sustained and emotionally charged attack on the agency.[5] The FSA was forced into a defensive position from which it had to fight for its very survival.

FSA programs were denounced as socialistic, unrealistic, and wasteful. "There is no place in history," declared Robert E. Short, president of the Arkansas Farm Bureau, "for a decent standard of living except on the basis of commercial agriculture." The FSA, he argued, "should be dismantled because it is perpetuating insidious and indefensible ideologies and socialistic experiments." However, it was not only the alleged socialism of the FSA which drew the heated criticism of Short and others; rather, it was also the success of the agency in converting tenant farmers and sharecroppers into successful independent farmers. One anonymous Arkansas critic of the FSA said of the agency:

> Well, it's this way. The government spends a million dollars or so to buy a 40-acre farm for a down-and-out sharecropper. They give him a mule, a bathtub and an electric shoelacer. They lay a railroad track to his house to carry the tons of forms he has to fill in. A bunch of experts figure out his milking I.Q., and behold, they teach his wife how to hook rugs, can beef and spinach, and they show the fellar how to plant soy beans and prune an orchard—and by damn, them government people can actually do it! After we poke fun at their red tape for a year or two, they ups and proves their experiment can pay itself off. . . . And I don't know who's more surprised, me or the cropper.[6]

Short stated the Farm Bureau's opposition to the FSA more bluntly when he said that "the FSA is causing large farmers to lose many of their best workers because money is being forced upon these people [tenants and sharecroppers] to buy farms and go out on their own." Some supporters of the bureau attacked the FSA more cleverly by charging that the cost of the war necessitated the curtailment of social programs. An editorial in the *Arkansas Democrat* called upon the government to terminate the program because "the cost of the war called for drastic economy and for the postponing of every social objective we can possibly get along without."[7]

Just as the FSA began to expand its services in order to increase wartime food production, the administration of President Franklin D. Roosevelt lost much of its congressional support during the off-year elections of 1942. The slow pace of the war, dissatisfaction with the rationing program, southern anger at the FEPC, the attempt to pass a federal anti-poll tax bill, and growing criticism of the FSA and other social programs were all factors in the Democratic losses. The new 78th Congress which convened in 1943 was controlled by a coalition of Republican and conservative anti-New Deal southern Democrats, and the FSA was one of the first New Deal reform agencies that was attacked. The charge was led by southern congressmen who had the strong support of the Farm Bureau. They not only wanted to kill the FSA, they also wanted to decentralize the Department of Agriculture.

The majority of critics of the FSA in the state were Farm Bureau members who operated huge plantations in the rich Mississippi delta lands of eastern Arkansas. These powerful Arkansans had never been strong supporters of the social programs of the New Deal, and when a bill was introduced into Congress to fund the FSA for 1943–1944, they urged their congressmen to work for its defeat. The chief representative of these interests in Congress was First District congressman Ezekiel C. "Took" Gathings of West Memphis who shared the views of the bureau. Much of the opposition to the FSA was economically motivated because the collective farming and loan programs operated by the agency cost large agricultural operators needed labor, but some of it was racially motivated. An example of the latter was found in Crittenden County in eastern Arkansas where black farmers, with the aid of the FSA, had organized a homestead association and employed both black and white women to do clerical work in the same office. The arrangement did not please both A. W. Oliver, the local county judge, and John A. Cooper, a local construction contractor. During the congressional debate over FSA funding for 1943–1944, they informed Congressman Gathings that "during the [election] year of 1944, this matter will be brought to light and could be detrimental to any candidate that might make the error of supporting the FSA to any degree."[8] Most of the critics of the FSA avoided direct reference to the racial policies of the agency and focused their attention instead upon the agency's loan and collective farming programs.

During the 1943 congressional debate over continued funding for the FSA, Gathings and other members of the Arkansas delegation were flooded with letters urging them to vote against the continuation of the agency. R. B. Shaw, one of Gathings' constituents and president of the Shaw Cotton Company of Marianna (Lee County), urged the congressman to vote against funding for all non-defense social agencies. "I think it very important that all non-defense spending should be stopped for the duration," Shaw wrote Gathings. "In fact I hope to see such agencies as the NYA, CCC, FSA, and quite a number of other Alphabetical Parasites eliminated. This seems a poor time to be experimenting with socialistic and communistic cure-alls." Others limited their criticism of New Deal reform programs to the FSA. C. F. Tompkins, president of the Mississippi County Farm Bureau, headquartered at Blytheville, Arkansas, urged Gathings to "use your influence to prevent FSA appropriations." The president of the Blytheville Chamber of Commerce also urged Gathings to fight for the elimination of future FSA funding. Anti-FSA letters and telegrams were also received by Representative J. William Fulbright of northwest Arkansas, but Fulbright was not as hostile toward the FSA as his eastern state counterparts.[9]

Most of the support for continued funding of the FSA came from its clients, public officials who had worked with the agency and believed that it provided needed services, and the few politicians who did not represent the Farm Bureau and its allies. Clients in Yell, Logan, Pope, and Conway counties pooled their meager resources during the congressional debate over FSA funding for 1943–1944 and purchased a full page advertisement in the *Arkansas Gazette* to defend the agency and encourage their congressmen to support continued funding. A Gentry family, beneficiaries of the FSA's small farm loan program, urged their congressman, J. W. Fulbright, to support the agency. "We say, do all you can to keep it as it is. Never let the Farm Bureau come in as it is working to do," they pleaded.[10] Support also came from John C. Pipkins, Arkansas commissioner of public welfare, who urged Congressman Gathings to "push for FSA funding because no agency, in my estimation, has done a more worthwhile job in our state." Pipkins' views were shared by Congressman Fulbright, but not by Gathings. Poultry and vegetable crops were the major industries in Fulbright's district, neither of which required the large volume of cheap labor that was needed on the cotton plantations in the eastern counties; therefore, he did not share the strong eastern Arkansas bias against the FSA.

In fact, he believed that many of the FSA's critics, "particularly Republicans and anti-New Deal Democrats are more interested in rapping the President than in the common good of our people." There were not, however, enough pro-FSA voices in the House to win, and the representatives voted against further funding of the FSA. Following House action, Congressman Gathings, who had assured members of the Arkansas Farm Bureau and other critics of the FSA that "I will do everything in my power to prevent increased FSA appropriations," wrote his constituents: "Congress has finally determined that it is going to . . . clean house of these socialistic and radical schemes fostered by New Deal agencies." [11]

The last hope of the FSA now lay in the United States Senate. Agency advocates petitioned state senators Hattie Caraway and John L. McClellan to support continued funding for FSA, but neither gave any indication how they would vote. However, by a voice vote the full Senate, over the objections of the Farm Bureau lobby and conservative southern Democrats, voted to fund the agency. The Senate appropriated $29,607,000 for FSA administration and authorized it to borrow $97,500,000 for rural rehabilitation loans and $30,000,000 for farm purchase loans for fiscal 1943–1944, a reduction of 36 percent. The cut had been orchestrated by the Farm Bureau lobby and the coalition of conservative anti-New Deal Democrats and Republicans in the Senate. This combination was also able to prevent passage of the reduced FSA appropriation bill until Calvin B. Baldwin, the liberal administrator of the agency, promised to resign. The Farm Bureau, which wanted to reduce the Department of Agriculture to nothing more than an advisory agency, was also successful in getting a rider attached to the appropriation bill of the AAA prohibiting it from publicizing itself or its achievements. In Arkansas and throughout the South, the ban on AAA promotional activities allowed the Arkansas Farm Bureau's Agricultural Extension Service, administered through the Department of Agriculture of the University of Arkansas, to promote itself without competition from the AAA. Nor could the FSA compete with the bureau's extension service because of its reduced appropriations. This was what small farmers and those with a desire to become small farm owners feared most. They accused the Farm Bureau of destroying the AAA and the FSA because "the Bureau wants small farmers and farm laborers for legalized slaves." [12] The members of the Arkansas Farm Bureau may not have wanted their smaller competitors for "legalized slaves," but the restriction placed on the FSA and the AAA by the 78th Congress greatly increased the ability of the bureau's supporters to maintain an ample supply of cheap labor.

The FSA lingered until 1946 when it was superseded by the Farmers Home

Administration. But after 1943, its effectiveness as a progressive agricultural reform agency had been severely curtailed. It was still able to provide limited services to its clients, but its ability to grant loans to tenant farmers and share-croppers to purchase small farms was almost totally destroyed by the budget cuts of the 1943 Congress. Furthermore, Arkansas planters made sure that the agency could not continue to operate its farm loan program in the state on its limited budget by sharply increasing the price of available agricultural property. A. D. Stewart, regional director of the FSA, cited Mississippi County in eastern Arkansas as the typical example of the rapid inflation of farm prices that occurred throughout the state after the agency's budget was cut. According to Stewart, Mississippi County had the largest percentage of farm tenancy in Arkansas and consequently received the greatest FSA appropriation for tenant farm purchases. But the agency could not purchase farms in the county for its clients because local landowners raised the price of available farms far above FSA approved limits. "Land values," complained Stewart, "were so high that it was unsafe for small farmers to buy and attempt to work out their indebtedness." [13] Big agriculture, through the Farm Bureau and its conservative Democratic allies in Congress, was able to minimize its competition. The small farmer, stripped of federal support, fell victim to the growing trend toward commercialized agriculture. Although World War II by itself did not destroy the small farmer, it greatly contributed to his demise.

Unions and the Right to Work

During the Second World War, organized labor in the United States made rapid gains. The fuel that powered the labor vehicle was the Wagner Act of 1935 which gave labor the right to organize and bargain collectively with management. It also forbade a number of unfair labor practices—among them the establishment of company unions. The Wagner Act was also a major stimulus for the organization of the CIO, which became the nation's largest industrial union. The Fair Labor Standards Act of 1938 also aided the growth of organized labor. It established minimum wage levels throughout the nation, stipulated a maximum forty-four hour work week, and abolished child labor. The fact that the administration of President Franklin D. Roosevelt was sympathetic to labor did not hurt its cause either. During the war, unions used their growing strength to push for higher wages, improved safety conditions, better fringe benefits, and the acceptance of the closed shop. When management refused to bargain in good faith, labor leaders resorted to their chief and most effective weapon—the strike. However, wartime strikes led to an outpouring of anti-union sentiment throughout the nation, even in those areas where unions had enjoyed good relations with management.

Arkansas had a relatively peaceful labor record during World War II. Between 1940 and 1944 there were only ninety-eight reported labor disputes in the state, and only seven of these involved work stoppages. None of these, reported Labor Commissioner W. J. McCain, were in war industries.[14] Despite this peaceful record, the majority of Arkansans were hostile toward unions. This attitude was due, in part, to union activity in the nation that patriotic Arkansans felt disrupted the national defense effort. They were especially distressed by John L. Lewis, head of the United Mine Workers union (UMW), when he called 400,000 bituminous coal miners out on strike in March 1941. Although the United States was not yet at war, Arkansans viewed the strike as a serious disruption of the national defense program. Reacting to the strike, the Batesville, Arkansas, branch of the American Legion adopted and forwarded to Congress a resolution urging the passage of anti-union, anti-strike legislation.[15] An editorial in the *Arkansas Gazette* accused Lewis of "being deaf to the voices of patriotic duty and blind to the perilous situation confronting America."[16] The anti-union sentiment cut across racial and ethnic lines in Arkansas. The black editor of the *State Press,* who usually took a pro-union position during labor disputes, also criticized Lewis and declared that "strikes play into the hands of Hitler and his associates and delay the preparedness of our nation to meet and victoriously halt their nefarious march of conquest."[17]

The public outcry against unions struck a responsive note in Congress. On December 3, 1941, the House passed an anti-union bill sponsored by Howard W. Smith, a Virginia Democrat. The Smith Bill would have forbidden all new closed shop agreements, denied Wagner Act benefits to unions with Communist or Bundist (German-American) officers, prohibited strikes without a majority vote of a union's membership, and provided for a thirty-day cooling-off period before a strike could be called.[18] The Senate, however, failed to act on the Smith Bill because of the confusion after the Japanese attack on Pearl Harbor four days later. Since there were no major strikes in 1942, Congress passed no relevant legislation, but anti-union opinions continued to escalate on the state level.

By 1942 anti-union sentiment in Arkansas was nearing its peak. The growing hostility toward unions was not because of major national strikes; it resulted rather from the attempt of the CIO to organize agricultural and domestic labor in the state. According to a CIO spokesman, the union planned to organize workers into closed shops from the coal fields of western Arkansas to the cotton fields of the eastern part of the state. Most of the coal miners belonged to the UMW union which was affiliated with the American Federation of Labor (AFL), leaving only the domestic and agricultural workers of eastern Arkansas for the CIO to organize. The majority of these were poor blacks who comprised the cheap labor pool of the state's large agricultural interests. Because the CIO did not exclude blacks from its ranks, the union was viewed in Arkansas as an advocate of racial equality—a foreign and dangerous concept. In a letter to Congressman E. C. Gathings, after Congress failed to pass anti-union legislation in 1941, Philip Hicky, owner and operator of the Fleurland Plantation in the eastern Arkansas county of St. Francis, said: "We have been working men for years and at no time have we ever had any labor trouble, but when these union organizers get hold of them, they make such fantastic promises. To my mind, one of the greatest injustices they are doing is to hold out social equality to the Negro . . . you can readily appreciate what it means when agitators get out among the Negroes and begin to preach social equality." [19] Gathings responded favorably. In March 1942, he delivered a speech on the floor of the House that called for the passage of strong anti-union legislation. Gathings blamed the Roosevelt administration and the labor department for the rise in union activity and said: "I believe that the immediate removal of Madam Frances Perkins as secretary of labor and the removal of Sidney Hillman, director of the labor division of the War Production Board, will bring unity out of chaos." The speech was just what Gathings' supporters wanted to hear. "I want to congratulate you on your speech on the floor of the House regarding labor," wrote R. B. Shaw, president of the Shaw Cotton Company in Marianna. "I am sure that a great majority of the citizens of the district [First Congressional] see 'eye to eye' with you." [20] Despite the efforts of Gathings and other anti-labor southern congressmen, Congress failed to pass any anti-union legislation in 1942, fearing that it would be vetoed by President Roosevelt in a congressional election year. The anti-union forces in Congress realized that the president would not endorse any legislation that might cost the Democratic party labor's vote.

When Congress failed to pass restrictive union legislation in 1942, large landowners decided in January 1943 to turn to the state legislature in an effort to curb organized labor. Their target was the CIO. The state's planters had not forgotten 1935 when the Southern Tenant Farmers Union, organized in 1934 in Tyronza, Arkansas, had successfully executed a cotton pickers strike in eastern Arkansas which forced plantation operators to raise the price of hand-picked cotton from 60¢ to 75¢ per hundred pounds, and they were determined not to repeat the experience. [21] Local agricultural businessmen also saw the activities of the CIO as a threat to the state's racial practices. Realizing that the legislature could not legally pass a law solely against the CIO, they used the war and the disruptive effects that strikes had on the war effort to try to get anti-union legislation passed in general. Because the legislature was controlled by the interests of big agriculture, they felt certain of success.

When the Arkansas General Assembly convened in January of 1943, the activities of the CIO in the state were the chief topics of debate. To curb the union's activities in the state, Senator W. H. Abington of Beebe sponsored Senate Bill No. 65, known as the Anti-Violence Law (or anti-strike bill). He opened debate on his measure by charging that the CIO was a Communist organization whose aim was "to cut the throat of organized labor in Arkansas and that the state could not submit to its domination." The bill made the use of violence or threats of violence in labor disputes, a felony punishable by up to two years in prison. By charging that the CIO was trying to destroy organized labor in Arkansas, Abington was apparently referring to the AFL, which had a good labor record in the state and was trying to assure AFL leaders that the measure was not directed at their union. If that was Abington's intent, it was not reassuring, because the measure brought strong criticism from all the state's labor organizations and their supporters in the legislature. Senator G. W. Lookadoo of Arkadelphia accused Abington of trying to ruin organized labor. Senator Leonard Barnes of Hamburg said the bill would only "stir up strife and conflict in Arkansas," and Senator Jim Snoddy of Mulberry said the Abington Bill was an injustice to labor. "It was unneeded legislation," declared L. P. Williams, secretary of the Arkansas AFL, "because organized labor in Arkansas has had a perfect record since the beginning of the war." However, it was Odell Smith, president of the Central Trade and Labor Council of Little Rock, who underscored the basic reason why the measure was introduced when he charged that "passage of this bill is being urged to prevent the organization of eastern Arkansas sharecroppers." After weeks of heated debate, the Abington anti-strike bill passed the Senate 20 to 12 and was sent to the House for final action.[22]

It was sponsored in the House by Representative W. O. Irby of St. Francis County in eastern Arkansas. Irby said he supported organized labor—presumably the AFL—but was opposed to the CIO because it represented "mass picketing, mass mayhem, and murder." Representative Julian James of Craighead County, also a self-claimed supporter of organized labor, argued for the Anti-Violence Law because he believed that "the CIO was attempting to take advantage of the small laboring man."[23] The measure provoked heated debate in the House because it only applied to employees and because many House members felt that the felony provision in the measure was too severe. After five hours of debate, opponents of the measure failed to amend the bill to eliminate the felony sentences and to make the bill apply to employers as well as employees; the statute passed 62 to 29 without any changes. Conservatives had won another victory. It came, however, only after "representatives of the Farm Bureau appeared at the legislature with little black grips," charged Jake Wilson of El Dorado, who was the AFL's labor representative in Arkansas and a former state senator.[24] Similar views were expressed by C. F. Byrns, editor of the *Southwest American* of Fort Smith. Byrns, who also wrote a daily column for the paper called "Off The Record," charged that the Abington Anti-Violence Law was doomed to failure until "prominent men from eastern Arkansas, whose voices speak with considerable authority in the legislature, came to Little Rock and put on the pressure." Governor Adkins, who also classified himself as a friend of organized labor, allowed the measure to become law without his signature. In explaining his actions to the public, he expressed confidence in the leaders of the AFL and commended it for its good record in the state, but said he could not veto the bill—as labor leaders had encouraged him to do—"without giving a free hand to unscrupulous agitators who attempt to organize domestic and farm workers."[25]

During the legislative debate over the Anti-Violence Law, the galleries of the House and Senate were filled with supporters of the measure who loudly cheered whenever defenders of the proposed legislation appeared to have won a point. The shouts and applause were so loud that when the Senate passed the measure, it took a five-minute recess to restore order.[26] The consensus among the majority of Arkansans was that unions were un-American, seriously hampered the war effort, and aided the enemy. "Organized labor," declared Ernest Borden, an irate Arkansan from Knobel, "is the curse of our war effort." Since organized labor in Arkansas was opposed to the Anti-Violence Law, some believed that they condoned violence. This view was revealed in a letter to the *Gazette* which asked, "Is the right to use violence, or threats of violence . . . one of the sacred prerogatives of organized labor, to be employed at their discretion? Is organized violence, or threats of such, any more sacred than unorganized or individual violence?"[27] Because of public support for the Anti-Violence Law, general anti-union sentiment allowed the state's large agricultural interests to seek the enactment of even more restrictive labor legislation; only a catalyst was needed. This was provided by the United Mine Workers union (UMW) in the spring of 1943 when it called a national strike against the coal industry.

Coal miners and other industrial workers were paid under the Little Steel Formula worked out by the War Labor Board (WLB) in January 1942. The formula recognized the forty-hour work week and the closed shop, but it limited wage increases to 15 percent above January 1941 levels. By 1943, union leaders were arguing that skyrocketing wartime inflation had destroyed most of the economic gains of labor and were demanding that the "Formula" be adjusted to compensate labor for its losses. In the interest of coal miners, John L. Lewis wanted the WLB to authorize a $2 per day wage increase, double pay for Sundays, broader vacation benefits, owner-provided safety equipment, and portal-to-portal pay. The last demand involved pay for the time—about one-and-one-half hours—spent traveling from the mine entrance to the site where the work for the day began. After two months of negotiations with the mine owners and WLB's failure to solve the issue, the UMW walked off the job when its contract expired at the end of April 1943. The WLB ordered Lewis to continue the negotiations and to call the miners back to work, but the union chief adamantly refused. "The miners," he said, "would not trespass on coal property without a contract." When Lewis refused to order the miners back on the job, the government took over the mines and placed them under Secretary of Interior Harold Ickes. But this did not settle the strike; it continued intermittently until October 1943, the month Lewis had stipulated as the final deadline for contract negotiations. By the end of the year Lewis had won a significant but costly victory for the UMW. The union won a basic pay increase of $2.18 per hour plus portal-to-portal pay. The strike, however, had caused immeasurable damage to the UMW and to organized labor in general.[28]

During the long UMW strike, Lewis became one of the most hated public figures in the nation. National public opinion polls showed that 87 percent of the people viewed Lewis unfavorably. *The Nation,* one of the country's more liberal magazines, said "the strike was irresponsible, unpatriotic, and unjustified no matter what the miners' grievances."[29] To the great majority of Arkansans Lewis had committed an act of treason by calling the strike during wartime. Describing it as "the most brazen, unpatriotic and flagrant example of sabotage ever called to the attention of the people," the United States Army Mothers Club of Arkansas telegraphed the president asking that Lewis and his followers be interned for the duration of the war. "No man," read the message in part, "is so big that he can withstand the heartbeats of the women who are the mothers and wives of men dying all over the world for this country." It was only natural for the mothers and wives of the men in uniform to protest disruptive strikes, but they were not the only ones to register strong protests. In June 1943, one month after Lewis called the UMW's strike, the Grant County (Sheridan) draft board announced that it would not draft any more men until the government put an end to strikes. The board also adopted and sent to the president a resolution urging him to "indict and try John L. Lewis and to order other draft boards to place in Class A all strikers, coal or otherwise." Resentment of Lewis and wartime strikes cut across all racial and socioeconomic lines in Arkansas. A black tenant farmer in eastern Arkansas, where blacks were more suppressed than in any other region in the state, placed his own depressed condition in the background by demonstrating his national patriotism through an anti-union letter to the editor of his local paper, the *Osceola Times*. He wrote:

> There may be a necessity of unions of many kinds at other times and places, but there should be but one union here which is the Union of the States and of the people to preserve such union, for victory can only be had through hard work, cooperation, and sacrifice; while on the other hand strikes and work stoppages may bring defeat.[30]

The people of Arkansas and the nation were willing to sacrifice the rights of organized labor in return for a victory over the World War II enemy.

Congress, irate with Lewis and also with President Roosevelt for his refusal to take forceful action against the UMW, reacted by opening debate on two anti-union bills. One was sponsored in the Senate by Tom Connally of Texas, the other in the House by Howard W. Smith of Virginia. The two statutes were combined by Congress, debated and passed as the Smith-Connally Act of 1943. The legislation gave the president more authority to seize industries useful to the war effort, made it a crime to encourage strikes in those industries, provided for a mandatory thirty-day cooling-off period before union leaders could call strikes, and forbade union contributions to political campaigns. The latter provision was an obvious attempt by conservative southern Democrats and Republicans to destroy the coalition between Roosevelt and organized labor which had been beneficial to both. President Roosevelt was caught in a dilemma. He wanted more power to curb wartime strikes but was opposed to the Smith-Connally Act because it threatened to cost him labor's support during the 1944 election. On June 25, 1943, the president attempted to solve his personal crisis by vetoing the bill and at the same time calling upon Congress to pass legislation that would authorize the government to draft strikers up to age sixty-five as noncombatants, but the government was in no mood to compromise and easily overrode the veto.[31] The entire Arkansas congressional delegation, to the satisfaction of their constituents, voted for the Smith-Connally Act and against the president. The state's agricultural interests had for some time been urging congressmen to seek passage of anti-union legislation, and the Smith-Connally Act received an overwhelming approval. "Just want you to know," wrote W. M. Freeze, an eastern Arkansas planter, to Congressman Gathings, "that the House and Senate action on the Smith-Connally Bill went over in a big way with everyone in this part of the country." [32]

For organized labor 1943 was not a good year. The passage of the Smith-Connally Act by Congress weakened the ability of unions to strike and to influence political action through economic contributions to the party they favored, and the passage of the Abington Anti-Violence Law by the Arkansas legislature virtually eliminated the strike altogether in the state. Since the law only applied to labor, management was free to use force to solve labor disputes, and the unions faced felony sentences if they retaliated in kind. However, many in the state did not believe that the anti-union legislation passed by Congress and the state legislature in 1943 went far enough. They wanted to free businessmen from the possibility of being forced into labor negotiations through a peaceful strike. Seeking to use the strong anti-union sentiment in Arkansas to their advantage, agricultural and business leaders, supported by the Christian Americans—a Texas-based group organized to promote passage of anti-labor legislation throughout the nation—and the state's timber interests, drafted and asked the voters to approve in the 1944 elections a "Right to Work Law" (Constitutional Amendment No. 35). The proposed law prohibited closed shops in Arkansas by eliminating union membership as a prerequisite for employment. It also forbade employers from entering into contracts that would deny employment to anyone who refused to join a union. [33] The state's lumber interests joined in the effort to get such a law passed because of increased union activity among its employees.

At the beginning of World War II in 1939, more than 60 percent of the land in Arkansas was covered by forests. Once the United States entered the conflict, the timber industry became the state's largest single employer. It was, however, according to investigators for the War Production Board (WPB) and the AFL, the most feudal in the nation. The Crossett Lumber Company, one of the state's largest, was also one of the worst. Describing the Crossett operations, J. P. McPherson, AFL organizer in Arkansas, wrote to William T. Schulte, the coordinator of field operations for the WPB: "I would say that they have always operated along the old feudal system and can't get the idea in their heads that the worker has any right to question what they are or are not given by the big industrial concerns." According to McPherson, the Crossett mills operated without regard to established health and safety standards. "I explained the origins and purpose of the Industrial Health and Safety laws," he reported to Schulte, "but I don't believe that this has ever meant much to the people in this part of the country."

In 1942, the Office of Price Administration (OPA) authorized a 50¢ per hour wage increase for timber workers, but the Crossett Company refused to pay the increased wage and when workers threatened to quit—many had military deferments secured by the company—the company threatened them with imprisonment. When AFL representatives attempted to organize the disgruntled workers, laborers were laid off and company officials, declaring that they suffered from a shortage of labor, requested the war department to allow them to use German prisoners of war. The use of German POWs, according to McPherson's report to the WPB, would have allowed the Crossett Lumber Company to fight successfully AFL attempts to organize its employees and force it to improve pay and working conditions.[34] Conditions in other Arkansas timber operations were no better.

Even more feudalistic in its operations than the Crossett Lumber Company was the Dierks Paper Company of Dierks, Arkansas. "The Dierks people," reported N. I. Callowick, regional labor representative for the WPB, "own and control every means of existence for inhabitants over a distance of at least fifty square miles. All of the necessities of life are controlled by them and in order for the people, who work and live on this Dierks property, to exist they are dependent entirely upon the Dierks interest." The Dierks company, like its Crossett counterpart, also claimed to suffer from a wartime labor shortage, and for the same reason: it wanted to curtail AFL organizational efforts by dismissing those employees who were union members. According to Callowick's report to the Office of Labor Production of the WPB, there were 1,500 people in the Dierks service area who were employed only on a part-time basis, and the local employment office had applications on file from "plenty of people who want to work but can't get it." Both McPherson and Callowick reported that there was no labor shortage in the Arkansas timber industry but that lumber companies were attempting to create artificial shortages to avoid using union labor and gain access to cheap prisoner-of-war labor. "It is quite evident," said Callowick, "that all the troubles of the lumber industry [in Arkansas] are directed specifically at eliminating union organization."[35] Owing the desire of Arkansas' feudalistic lumber industry to avoid unionization, which would have forced it to improve health and safety conditions on the job and pay at least a minimum wage, it is easy to understand why it joined forces with the state's planters to support passage of the proposed right to work law.

The "Right to Work Law" (Constitutional Amendment No. 35) was presented to the voters of Arkansas in 1944. It was promoted by its sponsors in such a way that it appeared to the average voter—most of whom were already strongly anti-union—that if it were not adopted, all workers in the state would be required to join a union as a precondition for employment. From the viewpoint of union spokesmen, Amendment No. 35 was a cowardly attack on organized labor. "I think the tactics used in this attack on organized labor," wrote Aubrey McCall, a Marine Corps veteran and a union member, "are about as low as the ones the Japs used at Pearl Harbor." An editorial in the same issue of the *Arkansas Gazette* that contained McCall's letter was also critical of the proposed constitutional amendment. The *Gazette* usually supported the interests of the state's agricultural and business leaders, but on this issue it broke away and urged voters to reject "such a vicious attack on organized labor." But the pro-"Right to Work" forces were too well-organized and financed to be deterred. They were able to capitalize on the strong wartime anti-union sentiment in the state, and in November 1944 voters overwhelmingly approved of the adoption of the "Right to Work Law" to the state constitution.[36] The opinion of most Arkansans was undoubtedly expressed by J. M. Evans in a letter to the *Gazette:* "Our boys over yonder are giving their lives for freedom—Hurrah for Amendment No. 35."[37] It mattered little to the state's majority that organized labor and Arkansas' unorganized working men and women had been denied a major avenue of upward mobility.

Organized labor in Arkansas emerged from World War II in a severely weakened condition. Not only were unions too weak to conduct successful strikes but closed shop agreements were not judged unconstitutional. They also failed between 1944 and 1966 to persuade the state legislature to adopt a minimum wage law.[38] During the war years, the state's conservative interests had effectively prevented the unionization of its cheap labor pool, and with the support of the timber interests, it had forestalled the incipient growth of strong unions in the state.

7 The Impact of War

On April 12, 1945, President Franklin Delano Roosevelt suffered a heart attack and died at his favorite vacation retreat in Warm Springs, Georgia. He was posing for a portrait. The picture was never completed, but the warm and smiling image of the president lived on in the hearts of the majority of his countrymen. The nation deeply mourned his death, but people realized that they could not drop everything for an extended mourning period because war was still being bitterly waged in Europe and Asia. Vice-President Harry S. Truman stepped in as the new leader of the nation and took the reins of the American war machine and continued the drive toward victory. He was unprepared for the role that was suddenly thrust upon him, but he matured into an able leader.

News of victory in Europe was flashed to the nation by radio on May 7, 1945. Normally, it would have been a time of tumultuous rejoicing, but the clamorous celebration that law enforcement officials throughout the nation expected did not materialize. In Arkansas a few factory whistles were blown in acknowledgment of the news, some mothers, fathers, wives, and sweethearts with loved ones on the European battlefields shed tears of gratitude, and some churches opened their doors for those who wished to offer a silent prayer. But there was no great outpouring of emotions or large victory celebrations as there had been at the end of World War I. The public realized that complete victory over Japan had not been won, and after a short pause, attention and energies were once again turned to the war in Asia and the production of war materials.[1]

In July 1945, President Truman, armed with the knowledge that American scientists had developed the world's first atomic bomb, warned the Japanese to surrender or risk complete annihilation. When the Japanese did not respond, the president authorized the use of the most destructive weapon of war ever invented. The decision to drop the atom bomb on Japan was not made lightly;

it was based on the belief that its use would save the lives of thousands of American servicemen and end the war quickly. On the morning of August 6, 1945, an atomic bomb equal in power to twenty thousand tons of TNT was dropped on Hiroshima. The explosion leveled most of the city, destroying an estimated eighty thousand people and seriously injuring thousands more. Japanese military officials, however, refused to surrender. Consequently, a second and more powerful atomic bomb was dropped on Nagasaki on August 9. The army still refused to concede but was overruled by Emperor Hirohito who notified the United States that his nation was ready to surrender. On August 14, 1945, an armistice was signed and on September 2, Japan formally surrendered. The Second World War, the most destructive and costly conflict in the history of mankind, was finally over; the time for rejoicing had come.

In Arkansas, state and local officials had carefully prepared for the wild celebration they expected to come with the announcement that the war with Japan had ended with victory. Their efforts were not in vain. When news of the armistice was announced in August, the festivities began. Liquor stores, as previously ordered, shut their doors, and other businesses voluntarily closed as their employees poured into the streets and performed victory dances to the sounds of automobile horns, factory whistles, cowbells, and the joyful shouts of men, women, and children. The four long years of war were over.[2]

World War II meant more than a military victory over Nazi Germany and Imperial Japan; the war had brought sudden and permanent changes to the socioeconomic character of the nation. During the war, the government had intervened into the domestic economy on a massive scale and permanently ended the commitment of the nation to *laissez faire;* the Full Employment Act of 1946 would commit the federal government to the economic prosperity and the social well-being of the American people. The war also produced or accelerated change in other ways: the trend toward commercial farming was greatly increased by wartime demands for foodstuffs, which signaled the beginning of the end for the small family farmer; it diversified the economy of many of the nation's rural agriculturally dependent areas; wartime medical development led to improved health care; it prepared the way for better education of the nation's citizenry through the passage of the GI Bill of Rights (the Serviceman's Readjustment Act); and the action of the federal government and the federal courts greatly expanded political and economic opportunities for blacks. Yet one of the many unanswered questions was whether the states would follow the lead of the federal government or whether they would seek a return to the status quo.

From Farms to Factories

World War II, combined with wartime directives from the federal government and progressive decisions handed down by the Supreme Court, forced Arkansas and its people to change many of their provincial political practices, but the economic changes caused by the war were the most far-reaching. Despite efforts by various New Deal agencies to relieve the impact of the depression on the nation, the majority of Arkansans were still suffering from the great economic collapse when World War II began. In 1939, there were 90,000 unemployed Arkansans, 67,000 were employed only part-time, and 30,000 were on the relief rolls of the state and federal governments. Thousands more had given up hope of finding employment and wandered around the state in despair.[3] However, the outbreak of the European conflict, the inauguration of a national defense program at home, and the eventual entry of the United States into the conflict ended the problems of unemployment and ushered in a new era of prosperity.

The long and lean depression years had denied many Arkansans consumer goods and services that were considered routine during normal times. Increased employment and income generated by the demands of war ended the self-denial. Beginning with the movement of national defense industries into Arkansas in 1940, Arkansans began an unprecedented spending spree. The urge to spend was revealed in growth statistics reported by major consumer industries in the state. The Arkansas Power and Light Company, the state's largest public utility, reported a dramatic expansion of services that were directly related to the increased income of the state's working population. In 1940, the utility reported 10,000 residential customers; by May of 1943 there were 74,000. In 1943, retail businessmen in Fort Smith reported a 27 percent increase in sales compared to the previous year. Little Rock businesses had a 12 percent increase for the same period. Similar reports came from cities throughout the state. The increase in consumer spending took place during the prewar national defense program and during the first year of World War II. Rationing of consumer goods and services began in 1942, and consumer spending declined quickly. Not all Arkansans spent their war-generated income; some made deposits in banks for future use. Between 1940 and 1943, bank deposits in Arkansas rose 128 percent.[4]

Increases in retail sales and bank deposits generally occurred in cities with war-related industries and represented one of the more significant changes that occurred in Arkansas during the war years—the movement of people from rural to urban areas. The population shift had a decisive impact not only on urban areas that were not equipped to handle the rapid growth but also on the state's agricultural industry which depended on a large pool of cheap labor. Of the 677,000 persons who comprised the farm work force in 1940, only 292,000 were left by the spring of 1944, and most of those that migrated to urban areas did not plan to return to farms after the war. An *Arkansas Gazette* survey questionnaire, given in 1945 to one-third of the employees in five of the war industries in Arkansas, revealed that 11.8 percent of the 20 percent of the people recruited from farms in 1940 classified themselves as skilled workers in 1945 and did not plan to return to agricultural employment after the war industries closed. This rural-to-urban migration forced the state's planters to shift from dependence upon an abundant supply of cheap human labor to the use of expensive machinery and hastened the development of commercialized agriculture in the state.[5]

With the rural-to-urban migration and the growth of large-scale commercialized farming in Arkansas during the war years, political and business leaders realized that there would no longer be a need for a large pool of cheap agricultural labor in the postwar years. They also understood that the state would need nonagricultural jobs if it was to maintain its population, the overall population of Arkansas having declined enough between 1940 and 1950 to cost the state one seat in the House of Representatives. The first step toward providing postwar jobs came in 1943 when Hamilton Moses, president of Arkansas Power and Light Company, and a group of the state's leading businessmen formed the Arkansas Economic Council (AEC), whose purpose was to formulate postwar plans that would allow war industries to convert to peacetime production and avoid a serious dislocation of the people and disruption of the state's economy. The AEC later merged with the state chamber of commerce and developed the "Arkansas Plan" which was an effort to balance agriculture and industry after the war. Business leaders made speeches throughout the state trying to gain support for more economic development, new chambers of commerce were formed, and counties and cities were encouraged to set up economic development committees.[6]

While the AEC was planning for Arkansas' postwar industrial development, other groups were unwittingly aiding its efforts. The Abington Anti-Violence Law passed by the 1943 legislature indirectly aided the goals of the AEC. The immediate purpose of the Anti-Violence Law, chiefly sponsored by the Farm Bureau, had been to curb the efforts of the CIO to organize agricultural and domestic workers in eastern Arkansas and force wage increases and better treatment. The measure was very effective, and in the long run the law made Arkansas quite attractive to northern and eastern industries that wished to relocate in the South in order to avoid the demands of organized labor. Although the AEC was unaware of the impact that the Anti-Violence Law would have on the state's postwar development, its presence on the statute books directly aided the council's program for postwar industrial development. However, the AEC had no immediate successes.[7]

In 1943, when the AEC was organized, major industries expressed no desire to locate in Arkansas. Although the council worked tirelessly to lure industries and to convince those that were in the state to continue operations after the war, it had little success. The infant AEC was simply unable to overcome the negative image of the state that had been generated for decades. In 1944, H. K. Thatcher, director of the Arkansas Agricultural and Industrial Commission, which maintained an office in Washington to seek investment capital, told state leaders that big investors were not willing to invest in the state because "they never know what Arkansas is going to do next." Ben Laney, elected governor in the 1944 general elections, told the Little Rock Chamber of Commerce that industrial growth had been slow because of "the fear that investors have that there will be some foolish legislation passed every time the legislature meets." Laney's comments were made in 1944, and the legislature, which only met in regular session every two years, was not scheduled to meet again until January 1945, at which time the governor planned to promote his own plan for the postwar industrialization of Arkansas. When the general assembly did convene in 1945, it created the Arkansas Resources and Development Commission (ARDC) and established an industrial bureau of research at the University of Arkansas. The ARDC and the bureau of research were given the joint task of identifying areas for industrial development and seeking new plants for the state.[8]

Prior to the meeting of the 1945 legislature, Arkansas' large agricultural interests, supported by lumber companies, made the next indirect but important move toward the industrial development of the state. In 1944, the two groups sponsored and the voters adopted a "Right to Work" constitutional amendment. "No person," read the amendment, "shall be denied employment because of affiliation with, or resignation from, a labor union, nor because of refusal to join or affiliate with a labor union." Combined, the Anti-Violence Law of 1943 and the "Right to Work" law of 1944 destroyed the ability of unions to organize effectively and allowed employers to ignore union demands by simply refusing to enter into binding contracts. Under such conditions Arkansas became very appealing to potential industrial investors. Although leaders of agricultural and timber interests were not interested in postwar industrial development, they had, through their determination to crush unions

and protect their cheap source of labor, indirectly prepared the way for industry to move into the state.[9]

Prosperity Without Social Gains

World War II brought an unprecedented economic boom to Arkansas and its people. The state's population enjoyed nearly full employment,
business and agricultural enterprises prospered, and for the first time in a de-
cade people were able to pay their state taxes which increased the financial
resources of state government. However, little of the increased revenues was
used to improve basic human services—housing, health care, and education.
Adequate housing, which had been a serious problem before the war, held that
same status after the war. According to a survey of postwar priorities conducted by the Arkansas Economic Council in March 1945, homes were first
on the list. Part of the housing problem was a result of wartime demands for
timber products, but that was not the major cause; Arkansas had never placed
a high priority on quality housing for its people. Consequently, there were few
vacant homes prior to the war. In 1940, the United States Census Bureau reported that the state had only 24,791 vacant dwelling units out of a total of
519,907, and vacancies had quickly disappeared once the defense boom began. As always, the poor were the ones who suffered most. In the fall of 1945,
the Pulaski County welfare department reported that welfare recipients were
being "forced to live in houses unfit for human habitation." There was little
relief in sight. In December 1945, W. C. Daniels, state director of the Federal
Housing Administration, reported that Arkansas needed a minimum of 5,000
new homes in 1946 just to begin to relieve the housing shortage.[10] Yet there
was no diligent effort by the state or private industry to improve housing, especially for the poor.

Not only did the poor suffer from the critical shortage of housing, but wartime demand for doctors and nurses had also deprived them of badly needed
medical care. There had been a prewar shortage of doctors numbering only
one for every 1,115 residents; by 1942 it was one for every 1,500 and the
shortage was increasing daily. The availability of trained nurses was also critical. By 1944, Arkansas had fewer nurses per civilian population than any
other state in the union. Fortunately, the federal government came to the res-
cue of the state's poor. In 1940, the government, in an attempt to help rural
states like Arkansas solve the problems of housing, education, and health care
caused by the rapid expansion of defense industries, established the Office of
Defense Health and Welfare Services as a division of the Farm Security Ad-

ministration (FSA), and by fall of 1941 it was operating a national health program for FSA clients. By 1945, the FSA had organized county medical associations in rural areas throughout the South. In Arkansas the FSA's health care program, which was organized in practically every county in the state, was administered through county health associations. Families paid a $12 membership fee to their local association plus $1 for each family member. The cost of medicine was not included, but doctors' office and house calls were covered."

The FSA's program was complemented by a federal maternal and infant care program offered to the wives of enlisted servicemen. The latter program was operated by the state Board of Health and provided free medical care to expectant mothers and to their children under one year of age. The state Board of Health, however, was forced to drop the federal program after a short period, because the Arkansas Medical Association (AMA) refused to cooperate with what it termed socialized medicine. Dr. W. R. Brooksher, AMA president, said the organization could not support the program because "it places a barrier between doctor and patient and establishes the base for a much larger federally controlled program to cover all classes of citizens." Fortunately for the future health of Arkansas infants there were enough doctors in the state willing to participate in the federal infant care program despite the position of the AMA to allow the board to revive the program in conjunction with the children's bureau of the U.S. Department of Labor. One result was that maternal deaths in childbirth in Arkansas had reached all time lows by 1943, and the infant mortality rate, which in 1936 was 7.3 percent for every 1,000 births, had fallen to 3.8 percent per 1,000 births in 1943. Educators have argued that a healthy child is an educable child, and the various health care programs operated in Arkansas during the war years by the federal government served to produce healthier children. Now it was up to the state to provide them with the educational opportunities they needed to be able to compete successfully in modern society.[12]

Public education in Arkansas had almost ceased to exist during the depression of the 1930s because of the economic crisis that confronted the state and because of its low priority. It was moving slowly up recovery road when the nation entered World War II, but the war brought this momentum to a halt and plunged public education in Arkansas and throughout the nation into another crisis period. The war brought industries to Arkansas, and most of these located in counties near populated areas but outside city limits, thereby placing heavy pressure on county schools. These were not as well financed as city schools and were unable to generate the capital needed from local sources to expand facilities to accommodate the influx of new students. Nor could the state provide county schools with relief. As early as 1940, rural school districts were told not to expect any state aid for the 1940–1941 academic year, and continued operation would have to depend upon tuition.[13] Not only were the schools unable to expand facilities, they were also unable to retain qualified teachers.

Few of the state's schools, rural or urban, were able to compete with the high-wage war industries for personnel; and faced with growing teacher shortages and poor financing, many were forced to close their doors. For the 1941–1942 school year, forty schools in Arkansas failed to open, and an additional seventy-five were forced to close after only two months of operation. In northwest Arkansas, teachers' salaries were so low that several schools were forced to shut their doors as teachers resigned to take jobs in the cotton fields of the Arkansas delta where they could make more money. Between 1940 and 1943, 100,000 of the state's 170,000 school age children between the ages of 13 and 18 did not attend school because there were no teachers or facilities available. Many older students migrated to defense areas in search of employment. By 1945, 47.8 percent of the labor force in Arkansas' war-related industries were high school or college age students. A survey of the postwar plans of former students, conducted by the Arkansas Economic Council in September 1945, revealed that only 2.5 percent of those questioned planned to return to school to complete their education. Even if any had desired to return to school to finish their education after the war, they would have found it difficult to find adequate facilities. In November 1945, only 445 of the state's 2,345 school districts were financially able to provide a minimum accredited high school education for their students.[14]

For those who remained enrolled in public schools during the war, the quality of education they received rapidly deteriorated. In 1940, there were 13,173 employed teachers in Arkansas with an average college preparation of 2.6 years. By 1945, over 50 percent had left the profession and 72 percent of their replacements had completed less than twelve semester hours of college work. Prospects were not bright for the postwar years. In 1945, Arkansas institutions of higher education produced only 436 teachers, many of whom had only completed the two years of college work required to receive a state teaching certificate. Moreover, there was no guarantee that these potential educators would remain in Arkansas, because salaries in the neighboring states of Missouri and Oklahoma were much higher. In fact, thousands of Arkansas teachers left the state during the war years for better paying jobs in neighboring states and for jobs in the war industries, and many of their former pupils planned to follow their example after completion of high school. A poll conducted by the *Tiger,* the school paper of Little Rock High School (the state's largest white high school which was later renamed Central High), on post-graduation plans for seniors in May 1945, revealed that 63 percent of the boys and 57 percent of the girls planned to leave Arkansas after graduation. The chief reason given was a lack of opportunity for employment and advancement.[15] This was what the Arkansas Economic Council, created in 1943, was working to prevent. If young whites saw few opportunities for advancement in postwar Arkansas, young blacks saw even fewer, since they were not as well educated as their white counterparts and had the additional problem of Jim Crowism to overcome.

Jim Crow: Alive and Well

The majority of blacks in prewar Arkansas were either unemployed or unskilled tenant farmers and sharecroppers, but the movement of industry into the state during the war with its demands for both skilled and unskilled labor resulted in new employment opportunities. Thousands of blacks left the farms for urban areas and jobs in the war industries. Many even left the state for employment in northern and eastern states, because industrial jobs in Arkansas were difficult to acquire at the beginning of the war years due to hiring policies that gave preference to whites. Between April 1, 1940, and November 1, 1943, Arkansas lost an estimated 10.9 percent of its population, and the majority of those who left the state were blacks. Those who remained in the state, however, were eventually able to find industrial employment, but the jobs came only after a severe wartime labor shortage forced Ed McDonald, regional director of the War Manpower Commission for Arkansas, Missouri, and Oklahoma, to order personnel directors at war industries in his region to hire women and minorities who had previously been denied employment and "to begin now—not tomorrow—to use these groups."[16]

Once blacks secured employment in the war industries, they seem to have been generally accepted "on the job" by their white co-workers. Employees, both white and black, focused on the defeat of the foreign enemies and pushed personal racial prejudices aside and developed a mutual respect for the skills and dedication of one another. "No person holds himself above the other workmen here," an employee of the Maumelle Ordnance Plant in Jacksonville told a "Run of the News" reporter for the *Arkansas Democrat.* "The democratic system here," he said, "has been perfected beyond all belief to an outsider." The editor of the *Pine Bluff Commercial,* commenting on the unity and spirit of workers at the Pine Bluff Arsenal, an incendiary bomb plant, declared that "the walls of prejudice in industry are crumbling for the simple and effective reason that the nation does not have enough manpower to do the job unless we utilize every available unit with utmost efficiency." However, for those opposed to equal employment the increased hiring of blacks was the result of President Roosevelt's creation of the Fair Employment Practices Committee (FEPC) in 1941 and not to the national demand for manpower.[17]

The FEPC, which prohibited racial discrimination in industries that held government contracts and in government-sponsored defense job-training programs, was established in response to black protests against job discrimination in the nation's defense industries and a threatened protest march on the nation's capital. It was not well received in Arkansas and other southern states. Most Arkansas whites saw the FEPC as an attempt by the federal government to force them to accept racial integration rather than as an agency designed to increase the economic opportunities of blacks. In an editorial attacking the equal employment guidelines of the FEPC, the *Southern Standard* of Arkadelphia called for the abolition of the agency because it was opposed to segregation. "There should be segregation," the paper editorialized, "because it makes for harmony and prevents racial friction." Similar sentiments were expressed by H. F. Jamison of Beebe, Arkansas, in a letter to the *Arkansas Gazette*. Jamison said the FEPC was interested in social, not economic, equality. He then spelled out what he believed that agency and its supporters stood for. Using the initials of the agency, Jamison said the FEPC stood for: "Foul Extremists Prefer Colored." The views of the FEPC expressed by the *Southern Standard* and Jamison were not those of isolated white supremacists in Arkansas; they were views shared by the state's white majority and their political spokesman. In a 1944 congressional speech opposing a one-year extension of the FEPC, Senator John L. McClellan said the agency should be abolished because when "whites and blacks are forced to work together it is an encroachment on the constitutional rights of both races." Representative J. William Fulbright, while campaigning for the United States Senate in 1944, told a cheering crowd at Marianna that he agreed with Senator McClellan. "I disapprove of legislation by Executive Order and such noble experiments as the Fair Employment Practices Committee. I am no New Dealer," he said. Fulbright won his 1944 race for the Senate and joined Senator McClellan in the fight against the FEPC. They argued that any attempt to improve the economic status of blacks would lead to a breakdown in the Arkansas tradition of white supremacy, and to the forced acceptance of racial equality.[18]

The United States Senate was still debating the extension of the FEPC when Fulbright took his seat as the Arkansas junior senator. He was soon flooded with letters from his constituents urging him to oppose any extension of the FEPC. Walter N. Turlock, president of the National Bank of Commerce in Pine Bluff, urged Fulbright to vote against the bill because "in my opinion his is a very vicious bill . . . it would hamper our development by creating racial prejudice and would open the door and encourage many thoughtless and vicious Negroes to demand racial equality." [19] Claude Sharpe of Little Rock, vice-president of the Scott Mayer Company, a grocery wholesale business, urged Fulbright to vote against a permanent FEPC because "you know the conditions down here as well as we do. The different races and colors never have blended together and never will." The senator received numerous similar letters from business and political leaders throughout the state and he assured them that "the Arkansas delegation has been united in opposition to this proposal" and that they would "work for the defeat of this much too drastic bill." In 1946, the bill to create a permanent FEPC was killed in the Senate by a southern filibuster. Once again, blacks' hope for postwar progress and entrance into the American mainstream had been sacrificed for the benefit of white supremacy in the South. An editorial in the *State Press* declared that the legislators had "capitulated to minority rule and misgovernment." [20]

The determination of white Arkansans to continue racial discrimination and segregation in the postwar era was not only demonstrated by the reaction of state political leaders to the bill to extend the FEPC, it was also revealed through the actions of state courts. In 1944, George H. Evans, a black Little Rock mortician, was called for jury duty in Pulaski County. Local papers reported that he was the first black called in the county in twenty years. Prejudice, however, proved to be alive still when the presiding judge waived the unity rule that required jurors to remain together during recess periods. The waiver meant that white jurors would not have to associate with a black on an equal basis.

The determination to observe the color line in race relations in legal and nonlegal matters was nowhere more clearly demonstrated than in the court of Municipal Judge J. A. Gallaher of Fort Smith, Arkansas. [21] In August 1944, two black women were brought before Judge Gallaher after being arrested for "entertaining" two white soldiers from New York who were stationed at nearby Fort Chaffee. The soldiers were released to military authorities and the women sentenced to 90 days in jail and fined $300 each. After announcing sentencing, Gallaher commented: "The people must not condone this color business." A few days later three black and two white men were brought before Gallaher on gaming charges; he imposed the maximum fines allowed, and again commented: "So far as it is in my power, don't expect any mercy when Negroes and white persons get to congregating together; the way to stop it is to give them everything in the book." [22] Although most courts in Arkansas were not as openly racist as Gallaher's, his decisions represented the position the state and its white citizens would take in postwar race relations.

The American victory over Japanese imperialism and German racism during World War II resulted in little change in the status of Arkansas blacks. Nationally, World War II represented a progressive turning point for the black experience in America, but Arkansas lagged far behind the rest of the nation in socioeconomic and cultural development. The persistence of racism forced blacks to enter the postwar era facing the same formidable obstacles they had confronted when the war began.

Notes

Chapter 1

1. *Fayetteville Daily Democrat* (Fayetteville, Arkansas), September 3, 1935.
2. Curtis Stahl, Jr. (Harrison, Arkansas), to the Editor, *Arkansas Gazette* (Little Rock), January 13, 1940. Hereafter, when letters to the editor are cited, only the author and town will be mentioned when letters originate from within Arkansas.
3. John L. Ferguson and J. H. Atkinson, *Historic Arkansas* (Little Rock, 1966), 294–301.
4. Editorial, *Fayetteville Daily Democrat*, January 4, 1940; *Pine Bluff Commercial* (Pine Bluff, Arkansas), February 7, 1940; Editorial, *Arkansas Gazette*, May 18, 1940.
5. Dr. F. W. Buercklin (Portia), to the Editor, *Arkansas Gazette*, April 9, 1940.
6. H. F. Rowland (Harrison), to the Editor, *Arkansas Gazette*, May 12, 1940.
7. Editorial, *Arkansas Gazette*, May 18, 1940.
8. P. N. Stephens (Little Rock), to the Editor, *Arkansas Gazette*, May 22, 1940.
9. Editorial, *Marked Tree Tribune* (Marked Tree, Arkansas), May 16, 1940.
10. *Arkansas Gazette*, May 31, 1940; George C. Couch (Bryant), to the Editor, *Arkansas Gazette*, June 1, 1940.
11. *Arkansas Gazette*, June 4, 1940.
12. *Arkansas Gazette*, May 23, 24, and June 1, 1940; *Northwest Arkansas Times* (formerly the *Fayetteville Daily Democrat*), May 24, 1940.
13. *Northwest Arkansas Times*, June 23, 1940.
14. *Arkansas Gazette*, June 23, and September 4, 1940; October 9, 1941.
15. Editorial, *Arkansas Gazette*, June 17, 1940.
16. *Arkansas Gazette*, July 13, 1940; Geoffrey Perrett, *Days of Sadness, Years of Triumph: The American People, 1939–1945* (Baltimore, 1973), 33–34.
17. *Arkansas Gazette*, June 3, 1940; *Northwest Arkansas Times*, August 12, 1940.
18. David E. Shannon, *20th Century America: World War II and Since*, vol. 3 (Chicago, 1974), 34–35.
19. William L. Langer and S. Everett Gleason, *The Undeclared War, 1940–1941* (New York, 1953), 2.

20. *Arkansas Gazette*, September 7, 1940; Editorial, *Northwest Arkansas Times*, August 20, 1940.

21. Editorial, *Southwest American* (Fort Smith, Arkansas, formerly *Southwest Times Record*), January 13, 1941; Editorial, *Benton County Democrat* (Bentonville, Arkansas), September 19, 1940.

22. Clyde T. Ellis to Dr. G. D. Counts (Wesley), Arkansas, March 3, 1941, Series 5, Folder 3, The Congressional Papers of Clyde T. Ellis, Mullins Library, University of Arkansas, Fayetteville.

23. Quoted in Perrett, *Days of Sadness, Years of Triumph*, 75; Richard B. Morris, et al., *America: A History of the People* (Chicago, 1971), 611.

24. Bern Carlock (Springdale), to Clyde T. Ellis, February 24, 1941, Ellis Papers, Series 5, Folder 3; William R. Runton (Little Rock), to Clyde T. Ellis, May 5, 1941; Laurence Witherspoon (Little Rock), to Clyde T. Ellis, February 24, 1941; Ellis Papers, Series 5, Folder 3.

25. John B. Walker (Jacksonville), to the Editor, *Arkansas Gazette*, February 20, 1941.

26. Letter to the Editor of the *Arkansas Gazette* over the signature of "100 Percent American," January 31, 1941.

27. J. H. King (Hot Springs), to the Editor, *Arkansas Gazette*, March 30, 1941.

28. E. A. Teague (Piggott), to the Editor, *Arkansas Gazette*, May 21, 1941.

29. *Benton County Democrat*, November 13, 1941.

30. John M. Blum, et al., *The National Experience: A History of the United States*, 3rd ed. (New York, 1973), 663, 675.

31. Shannon, *20th Century America*, 457.

32. Shannon, *20th Century America*, 42.

33. Editorial, *Northwest Arkansas Times*, December 2, 1940; *Northwest Arkansas Times*, August 6, 1941.

34. From a congressional speech by Clyde T. Ellis, May 5, 1941, Copy in Ellis Papers, Series 4, Folder 2; Editorial, *Arkansas Gazette*, November 30, 1941.

35. Perrett, *Days of Sadness, Years of Triumph*, 190.

36. Editorial, *Arkansas Gazette*, December 8, 1941.

37. *Benton County Democrat*, December 11, 1941; *Arkansas Gazette*, December 9, 1941; *Jonesboro Evening Sun* (Jonesboro, Arkansas), December 10, 1941; *Arkansas Gazette*, December 19, 1941.

38. D. Y. Griffin (Little Rock), to the Editor, *Arkansas Gazette*, April 12, 1942.

39. Mrs. E. B. Stevenson (Kensett), to the Editor, *Arkansas Gazette*, May 22, 1942.

40. Editorial, *Arkansas State Press*, Little Rock, June 12, 1942. The *Arkansas State Press* was a black weekly that began publishing in Little Rock, Arkansas, on May 9, 1941, and ran continuously until October 30, 1959. It was the only black paper that had a statewide circulation with a predominantly white audience. Hereafter, *Arkansas State Press* will be cited as *State Press*.

41. *Arkansas Gazette*, January 2, 1942; *Pine Bluff Commercial*, May 28, 1942.

42. *Arkansas Gazette*, July 12, 1942.

43. *State Press*, December 12, 1941.

44. *Arkansas Gazette*, April 11, 1942; *Marked Tree Tribune*, May 6 and 13, 1943.

45. *Arkansas Gazette*, December 13, 1941; *Jonesboro Evening Sun*, December 18, 1941; *Arkansas Gazette*, December 19, 1941.

46. *Jonesboro Evening Sun*, April 9 and June 12, 1942.

47. *Northwest Arkansas Times*, April 25, 1942.

48. *Arkansas Gazette*, January 10, 1943; *Jonesboro Evening Sun*, December 18, 1941; *Arkansas Gazette*, February 14, 1943.

49. *Jonesboro Evening Sun*, July 9, 1940; *Arkansas Gazette*, March 10 and April 1, 1943.

50. *Arkansas Gazette*, October 18, 1943; *Marked Tree Tribune*, April 23, and November 26, 1942.

51. *Arkansas Gazette*, January 23, 1942; *Arkansas Democrat* (Little Rock, Arkansas), June 19, 1942.

52. *Arkansas Gazette*, October 28, 1943; *Jonesboro Evening Sun*, December 2, 1943.

53. *Arkansas Gazette*, September 10, 1943.

Chapter 2

1. See report of Denton O. Rushing, farm placement supervisor in general records for Farm Placement Service–Arkansas, May, 1942, War Manpower Commission, Record Group 211, Box 16, National Archives, Washington D.C.; James Emmet P. Griner, "The Growth of Manufacturing in Arkansas, 1900–1950" (George Peabody College for Teachers, unpublished Ph.D. Dissertation, 1957), 161.

2. *Arkansas Gazette*, September 8, 1940.

3. From Eugene Newsom, "What's Wrong with Arkansas," *American Mercury Magazine* (May 1954): 41; also see, Foy Lisenby, "A Survey of Arkansas' Image Problem," *Arkansas Historical Quarterly*, 30 (Spring 1941): 60.

4. Thomas W. Jackson, *On a Slow Train through Arkansas* (Chicago, 1942); *Arkansas Gazette*, September 8, 1940.

5. Griner, "The Growth of Manufacturing in Arkansas," 161.

6. United States Employment Service (USES), Department of Labor, Area Labor Market Survey Reports–Arkansas, March 13, 1942, National Archives, Washington, D.C. Hereafter cited as USES Labor Survey Reports.

7. Ferguson and Atkinson, *Historic Arkansas*, 301; Griner, "The Growth of Manufacturing in Arkansas," 167.

8. *Arkansas Gazette*, November 10 and 13, 1940; Editorial, *Pine Bluff Commercial*, October 31, 1940.

9. USES Labor Survey Reports–Arkansas, December 9, 1941.

10. *Southwest Times Record*, January 4, 1942; *Arkansas Gazette*, December 22, 1940; *Arkansas Democrat*, January 4, 1942; *Arkansas Gazette*, December 27, 1941; *Pine Bluff Commercial*, July 5, 1942; personal interview with Marshall Matthews, September 14, 1977. Mr. Matthews served as a research chemist at the Pine Bluff Arsenal from 1942 to 1946. He is currently employed by Arkansas State University, Jonesboro, Arkansas.

11. *Arkansas Gazette*, March 5 and 22, 1942; *Pine Bluff Commercial*, May 3 and July 5, 1942.

12. *Arkansas Gazette*, November 10, 1940.

13. Ferguson and Atkinson, *Historic Arkansas*, 301; *Arkansas Gazette*, November 30, 1940.

14. *Arkansas Gazette*, November 30, December 15, and December 8, 1940.

15. *Arkansas Gazette*, December 13 and 23, 1940.

16. *Jonesboro Evening Sun*, June 12, 1942; *Southwest American*, October 2, 1941.

17. *Arkansas Gazette*, September 7, 1943.

18. *Southwest American*, April 8, 1942; USES Labor Survey Reports–Arkansas, December 9, 1941; *Arkansas Democrat*, January 1 and September 6, 1942; *Pine Bluff Commercial*, September 6, 1942.

19. *Arkansas Gazette*, March 22 and April 4, 1942; *Hope Star* (Hope, Arkansas), April 24, 1942.

20. *Arkansas Democrat*, July 15, 1943; *Pine Bluff Commercial*, July 22, 1943.

21. *Arkansas Democrat*, October 24, 1943.

22. *Arkansas Democrat*, November 9, 1943.

23. USES Labor Market Survey Reports–Arkansas, Department of Labor, May 28, 1945, Box 18.

24. *Arkansas Gazette*, August 15, 1942.

25. *Arkansas Gazette*, May 30, 1942.

26. *Arkansas Democrat*, March 18, 1944; *Arkansas Gazette*, March 17, 1944.

27. Editorial, *Arkansas Gazette*, March 22, 1944.

28. *Arkansas Democrat*, May 25, 1945; *Arkansas Gazette*, March 1, 1942.

29. *Atkins Chronicle* (Atkins, Arkansas), February 18, 1944; *Arkansas Gazette*, February 16, 1944; Ferguson and Atkinson, *Historic Arkansas*, 305–306; *Marked Tree Tribune*, June 11, 1942; *Jonesboro Evening Sun*, October 23, 1942.

30. *Atkins Chronicle*, October 16, 1942.

31. *Arkansas Gazette*, November 1, 1942; *Arkansas Democrat*, January 3, 1943.

32. *Arkansas Gazette*, September 1, 1942; Editorial, *Arkansas Democrat*, September 6, 1942; *Arkansas Gazette*, September 6, 1942.

33. *Arkansas Gazette*, March 17, 1940.

34. *Arkansas Gazette*, unsigned letters to the Editor, February 26 and March 16, 1940.

35. Mary Robinson, "Women Workers in Two Wars," *Monthly Labor Review*, 57

(October 1943): 652; *Arkansas Gazette*, June 10, 1943; *Arkansas Democrat*, July 11, 1943.

36. Griner, "The Growth of Manufacturing in Arkansas," 161.

37. *Arkansas Gazette*, "Sunday Magazine," March 1, 1942.

38. *Arkansas Gazette*, March 22, 28, and May 10, 1940; *Arkansas Democrat*, March 21, 1942.

39. *Northwest Arkansas Times*, April 3, 1942; *Arkansas Gazette*, January 6 and May 5, 1943; *Pine Bluff Commercial*, June 14, 1942.

40. *Pine Bluff Commercial*, March 22 and February 21, 1943; *Pine Bluff Commercial*, February 21, 1943.

41. *Arkansas Gazette*, September 17, 1942; *Southwest American*, January 23, 1943.

42. *Arkansas Gazette*, April 19 and May 31, 1942; Editorial, *Pine Bluff Commercial*, January 4, 1943.

43. Mrs. Otto Whittington (Springdale), to the Editor, *Arkansas Gazette*, May 31, 1942.

44. *Southwest American*, June 8, 1945; *Arkansas Gazette*, May 12, 1943 and December 31, 1944.

45. *Pine Bluff Commercial*, July 25, 1942.

46. United States Department of Labor, Women's Bureau. *State Minimum Wage Laws and Orders*, July 1, 1942–July 1, 1950, Bulletin 191 (1950), 6, chapter 3.

Chapter 3

1. *Arkansas Gazette*, December 1, 1942, and March 27, 1943.

2. Report of Denton O. Rushing, farm placement supervisor, War Manpower Commission, Department of Labor, May 1942, Farm Placement Service–Arkansas, Record Group 211, National Archives (Hereafter cited as RG211); *Marked Tree Tribune*, March 14, 1940; *Northwest Arkansas Gazette*, June 10, 1942; *Arkansas Gazette*, January 23, 1942; *Benton County Democrat*, February 19, 1942.

3. *Public Education in Arkansas: A Survey* (Little Rock: Public Expenditure Council, 1945), 39. The council was composed of a conservative group of Arkansas businessmen who conducted a study of agricultural income in Arkansas to determine if the state's population had the capital needed to support increased funding for the public school system.

4. *Arkansas Gazette*, February 12, 25, and March 28, 1943; *Southwest American*, June 17, 1943.

5. *Arkansas Gazette*, December 14, 1942.

6. *Arkansas Gazette*, April 15 and July 21, 1943.

7. *Southern Standard* (Arkadelphia, Arkansas), December 3, 1942; *Northwest Arkansas Times*, December 12, 1940; *Arkansas Democrat*, December 13, 1940; *Arkansas Gazette*, October 10, 1943; *Southern Standard*, February 18, 1943.

8. *Northwest Arkansas Times*, July 25, 1944; *Arkansas Democrat*, May 13, 1945.

9. *Arkansas Gazette,* January 10 and 18, 1942.

10. *Arkansas Gazette,* January 19 and March 9, 1943.

11. Editorial, *Marked Tree Tribune,* December 10, 1942; Charlie Walters (Atkins), to the Editor, *Atkins Chronicle,* June 19, 1942. Hereafter only the place of origin of a letter to the editor will be cited when letters were mailed from within Arkansas.

12. T. M. Stinnett and Clara B. Kennon, *All This and Tomorrow Too: The Evolution and Continuing History of the Arkansas Education Association* (Little Rock, 1969), 171–172; *Arkansas Gazette,* January 6 and 13, 1935; Ferguson and Atkinson, *Historic Arkansas,* 338; *Fayetteville Daily Democrat,* July 19, 1935; David E. Rison, "Arkansas During the Great Depression" (University of California, Los Angeles, unpublished Ph.D. Dissertation, 1974), 81; Editorial, *Journal of Arkansas Education* (January 1937): 2.

13. *Hope Star,* April 24, 1942; "Recent Migration into Fort Smith, Arkansas," *Memorandum,* December 9, 1941; United States Employment Service, Area Labor Market Survey Reports–Arkansas, Record Group 183, National Archives.

14. *Arkansas Gazette,* February 6, 1940.

15. *Arkansas Gazette,* December 15, 1940.

16. *Northwest Arkansas Times,* November 11 and 18, 1940; *Arkansas Gazette,* August 24, 1941, and July 4, 1943; *Southern Standard,* November 21, 1940.

17. *Public Education in Arkansas: A Survey,* 46.

18. Stinnett and Kennon, *All This and Tomorrow Too,* 181; *Southwest Times Record,* February 11, 1940; *Arkansas Gazette,* October 2 and December 24, 1942; *Arkansas Democrat,* October 21, 1943.

19. Gerald D. Nash, *The Great Depression and World War II: Organizing America, 1933–1945* (New York, 1979), 147; Perrett, *Days of Sadness, Years of Triumph,* 338; *Arkansas Gazette,* May 12, 1943.

20. *Arkansas Gazette,* April 17, 1943.

21. *Public Education in Arkansas: A Survey,* 48–49; Editorial, *Arkansas Gazette,* April 17, 1943.

22. *Arkansas Gazette,* October 21, 1943; *Arkansas Democrat,* October 21, 1943.

23. *Arkansas Gazette,* March 1, 1942.

24. *Arkansas Gazette,* October 21 and 24, 1943, and January 5, 1944.

25. Editorial, *Arkansas Democrat,* October 24, 1943; "The Arkansas Story," Address of Governor Ben Laney to the Arkansas Educational Association, November 10, 1945, *Journal of the Arkansas Education Association,* vol. 19 (December 1945): 8–10.

26. Stinnett and Kennon, *All This and Tomorrow Too,* 191; *Arkansas Democrat,* November 15, 1945.

27. *Southwest American,* January 8, 1944; *Arkansas Gazette,* November 19, 1945; *Journal of Arkansas Education,* 19 (December 1945): 35.

28. Nash, *The Great Depression and World War II,* 147.

29. *Arkansas Gazette,* September 1, 1942; Editorial, *Arkansas Democrat,* September 6, 1942.

30. *Pine Bluff Commercial*, January 30, 1940; *Northwest Arkansas Times*, January 30, 1940. The majority of the information in this chapter has previously been published by the author in the *Arkansas Historical Quarterly*, 39 (Spring 1980): 20–34, and is reprinted here with the permission of the editor of the *Quarterly*.

31. *Jonesboro Evening Sun*, February 3, 1941; *Arkansas Gazette*, July 9, 1941; *Southwest Times Record*, January 18, 1941.

32. *Pine Bluff Commercial*, January 13, 1942.

33. *Arkansas Gazette*, August 30, 1942.

34. *Arkansas Gazette*, April 1, 1943.

35. *Pine Bluff Commercial*, February 14, 1943; Editorial, *Arkansas Democrat*, September 1, 1942.

36. *Arkansas Gazette*, May 11, 1943, and August 1, 1944.

37. *Arkansas Gazette*, April 21, 1944; *Southwest American* (formerly the *Southwest Times Record*), August 15, 1944.

38. *Jonesboro Evening Sun*, February 2, 1943; *Arkansas Gazette*, October 2 and 12, 1943, and September 6, 1944; *Southwest American*, September 6, 1944.

39. *Arkansas Gazette*, January 5, 1942; *Northwest Arkansas Times*, January 21, 1942.

40. *Arkansas Gazette*, July 30, 1943, and September 6, 1944.

41. *Arkansas Gazette*, September 25 and November 5, 1943, and February 4, 1945.

42. Editorial, *Arkansas Gazette*, April 3, 1940.

43. *Arkansas Democrat*, January 1, 1941; *Arkansas Gazette*, January 3, 1941.

44. *Arkansas Gazette*, February 5, 1941.

45. *Arkansas Gazette*, February 13 and March 6, 1941; *Arkansas Democrat*, March 5 and 6, 1941.

46. *Arkansas Gazette*, February 6, 11, and March 6, 1941.

47. *Arkansas Gazette*, January 29 and March 6, 1941; *Arkansas Democrat*, March 5, 1941.

48. Editorial, *Arkansas Gazette*, February 26, 1941.

49. *Arkansas Gazette*, March 29, 1941; *Arkansas Gazette*, May 12, 1943.

50. *Arkansas Democrat*, January 2, 1944; *Arkansas Gazette*, December 31, 1944; the term "gangplank marriage" was used by sociologists to describe marriages contracted by soldiers on the eve of departure for camp or overseas service.

51. *Southwest American*, May 5, 1944; *Arkansas Democrat*, July 16, 1944.

52. *Southwest American*, January 28, 1945; *Arkansas Gazette*, January 24, 28, and February 1, 1945; *Arkansas Democrat*, January 25 and 26, 1945.

53. *Arkansas Gazette*, February 1, 20, and March 13, 1945; *Southwest American*, January 28, 1945; *Arkansas Gazette*, March 13, 1945.

54. *Arkansas Gazette*, February 6, 1945; *Arkansas Democrat*, February 16, 1945.

55. *Arkansas Gazette*, February 6 and May 25, 1945; *Arkansas Democrat*, February 16, 1945.

Chapter 4

1. *An Act to Provide for the Common Defense by Increasing the Personnel of the Armed Forces of the United States and Providing for Its Training,* United States Congress, Publication L. 783, 76th Congress, Second Session, 1940, U.S. Statistics at Large, 844. Hereafter cited as the Selective Service Act of 1940.

2. Exodus, 20:4 and 13 (King James Version).

3. *Jehovah's Witnesses and the War* (New York: American Civil Liberties Union, 1943), 7.

4. Perrett, *Days of Sadness, Years of Triumph,* 91; Richard Polenberg, *War and Society: The United States, 1941–1945* (New York, 1972), 59–60.

5. Polenberg, *War and Society,* 59.

6. *Arkansas Gazette,* June 11, 1940; *Jonesboro Evening Sun,* June 13, 1940; Editorial, *Sharp County Record* (Evening Shade, Arkansas), June 14, 1940; Cluster Thomas, (Pangburn), to the Editor, *Arkansas Gazette,* September 1, 1941. Hereafter, when letters to the editor are cited, only the author and town will be mentioned when letters originate from within Arkansas.

7. *Arkansas Gazette,* June 30, 1940.

8. *Arkansas Gazette,* December 10, 1941, and March 29 and June 9, 1942; *Marshall Mountain Wave* (Marshall, Arkansas), June 12, 1942.

9. *Arkansas Gazette,* June 16, 1942; *Northwest Arkansas Times,* June 16, 1942; *Pine Bluff Commercial,* June 16, 1942. In his dissenting opinion, Chief Justice Smith said he believed that Johnson's actions resulted more from ignorance than from a deliberate expression of contempt for the flag. Declaring that he lacked sympathy for Johnson's attitude but respected his rights, Smith wrote: "If ignorance was a legal crime the judgment would be just. But witch-hunting is no longer sanctioned . . . we are engaged in a war wherein liberty may be lost if we succumb to the ideologies of those who enforce obedience through fear and who write loyalty with a bayonet."

10. *Arkansas Gazette,* January 11 and February 19, 1942.

11. *Jehovah's Witnesses and the War,* 10; *Arkansas Gazette,* September 16, 17, and 18, 1942.

12. *Jehovah's Witnesses and the War,* 10; *Arkansas Gazette,* September 21, 1942; *Pine Bluff Commercial,* September 21, 1942; *Arkansas Democrat,* September 21, 1942; Oscar A. Hays, Deputy Sheriff (Camden), to the Editor, *Arkansas Gazette,* September 23, 1942.

13. *Arkansas Gazette,* September 21, 23, and October 4, 1942.

14. Selective Service Act of 1940; *Jehovah's Witnesses and the War,* 7.

15. C. Calvin Smith, "Homer M. Adkins: Arkansas' Wartime Governor," in *The Governors of Arkansas,* eds., Timothy P. Donovan and Willard B. Gatewood, Jr. (Fayetteville, 1981), 190; Woody A. Tomlinson (Fayetteville), to the Editor, *Northwest Arkansas Times,* December 17, 1941; interview with Jehovah's Witness Dale Thiede, conscientious objector, WWII, Little Rock, Arkansas, November 10, 1983.

16. All of the information on the case of Albert H. Blakely was taken from a letter sent by him to General Lewis B. Hershey, national director of Selective Service, in June 1943. The letter requested the restoration of Blakely's IV–D classification and described the treatment that he had received from his local draft board. A xeroxed copy is in the possession of the author. Hereafter this material will be cited as Blakely Correspondence.

17. Mulford Q. Sibley and Philip E. Jacob, *Conscription of Conscience: The American State and the Conscientious Objector, 1940–1947* (New York, 1952), 70–71; Blakely Correspondence; Selective Service System, *Selective Service and Victory: Fourth Report of the Directory of Selective Service, 1944–1945* (Washington, 1948), 423.

18. *Arkansas Gazette,* March 9, 1943; Polenberg, *War and Society,* 60; Perrett, *Days of Sadness, Years of Triumph,* 366.

19. John M. Blumm, *V Was for Victory: Politics and American Culture during World War II* (New York, 1976), 155; Nash, *The Great Depression and World War II,* 156; Polenberg, *War and Society,* 71.

20. Guy E. Dorr, "Issei, Nisei, and Arkansas: A Geographical Study of the Wartime Relocation of Japanese-Americans in Southeast Arkansas," (University of Arkansas, Fayetteville, unpublished M. A. thesis, 1977), 24–25; Dillon S. Meyer, *Uprooted Americans* (Tucson, 1971), 22; Perrett, *Days of Sadness, Years of Triumph,* 91; quoted in Polenberg, *War and Society,* 62.

21. Merton Grodzins, *Americans Betrayed: Politics and the Japanese Evacuation* (Chicago, 1949), 17; Meyer, *Uprooted Americans,* 22; Nash, *The Great Depression and World War II,* 156; *Saturday Evening Post,* May 9, 1942; quoted in Nash, *The Great Depression and World War II,* 156; quoted in Polenberg, *War and Society,* 63.

22. "Executive Order No. 9066," John L. DeWitt, U.S. Army, Western Defense Command and Fourth Army, Final Report, *Japanese Evacuation from the West Coast, 1942* (Washington, 1943), 6; Blum, *V Was for Victory,* 155–156; Nancy Sparks, "Tragic Artwork from Rohwer," *Arkansas Gazette,* October 3, 1979, 3b and 8b; Polenberg, *War and Society,* 70.

23. *Arkansas Gazette,* June 3, 1942; *Pine Bluff Commercial,* June 8 and 12, 1942; Sparks, "Tragic Artwork from Rohwer," 8b; Dorr, "Issei, Nisei, and Arkansas," 184; Ruth P. Vickers, "Japanese-American Relocation," *Arkansas Historical Quarterly,* 10 (Summer 1951): 170–198.

24. The Personal Narrative of Ray D. Johnston, project director, Rohwer, War Relocation Authority (Little Rock: Arkansas History Commission). Mr. Johnston worked at the Rohwer relocation center from September 18, 1942, to December 31, 1945. Hereafter cited as Johnston Narrative; Austin Smith, Reports Division, Rohwer, War Relocation Authority (Little Rock: Arkansas History Commission). Mr. Smith served as the Rohwer Reports Officer from October 27, 1942, to December 31, 1945. Hereafter cited as Smith's Report.

25. William C. Anderson, "Early Reaction in Arkansas to the Relocation of Japa-

nese in the State," *Arkansas Historical Quarterly,* 23 (Autumn 1964): 198; Vickers, "Japanese-American Relocation," 170; Edgar V. McCoy, community analyst, Jerome, Field Report No. 15, August 20, 1943. War Relocation Authority, community analyst section, Record Group 210, Box 17, Folder 2, National Archives. Hereafter cited as McCoy Reports.

26. Homer M. Adkins to J. H. Tolan, chairman, House committee investigating national defense migration, February 27, 1942, Office Correspondence, Section III, A, Folder 78. The Papers of Governor Homer M. Adkins, Arkansas History Commission, Little Rock. Hereafter only names, dates, and locations of correspondence will be cited.

27. Dorr, "Issei, Nisei, and Arkansas," 36; *Arkansas Gazette,* February 28, 1942; E. B. Whitaker to Milton Eisenhower, director, WRA, April 17, 1942. A copy of this letter is located in the Adkins Papers, Office Correspondence, Section III, A, Folder 78; Robert A. Leflar, War Relocation Authority—Attorney to Philip Glick, January 4, 1942, File Box 4, Folder 20, Robert A. Leflar Papers, University of Arkansas Library, Fayetteville.

28. *Northwest Arkansas Times,* April 7, 1942; *Arkansas Gazette,* April 7, 1942.

29. Jones to Adkins, July 11, 1942, Office Correspondence, Section III, A, Folder 78, Adkins Papers; *Arkansas Gazette,* July 12, 1942.

30. *Arkansas Gazette,* June 4, 1942; also see P. E. Toler (Little Rock) to the Editor, *Arkansas Gazette,* August 4, 1942.

31. *Arkansas Gazette,* June 3 and July 2, 1942; Quoted in *Saturday Evening Post,* May 9, 1942; Editorial, *Arkansas Democrat,* June 21, 1942; *McGehee Times* (McGehee, Arkansas), June 25, 1942.

32. Editorial, *Southern Standard,* June 4, 1942; Walter N. Vernon, *Methodism in Arkansas, 1816–1976* (Little Rock, 1976), 310.

33. Vernon, *Methodism in Arkansas,* 310.

34. *Arkansas Gazette,* September 29 and December 2, 1942; *McGehee Times,* October 1, 1942; Anderson, "Early Reaction in Arkansas to the Relocation of Japanese in the State," 203.

35. Lowell to Glick, February 25, 1943, Leflar Papers, File Box 4, Folder 20.

36. *Arkansas Gazette,* September 24, October 21, and 30, 1942.

37. *Arkansas Gazette,* November 8, 1942; *McGehee Times,* November 12, 1942; *Arkansas Gazette,* January 10, 1943.

38. *Arkansas Gazette,* December 4, 1942, and May 6, 1943; *Pine Bluff Commercial,* May 5, 1943; I. C. Oxner to Adkins, January 9, 1943; Adkins to Oxner, January 11, 1943; Adkins to War Relocation Authority (draft letter, no date), Adkins Papers, General Correspondence, Section III, A; Ex-U. S. Soldier to Adkins, December 7, 1942, Office Correspondence, Section III, A, Folder 78, Adkins Papers.

39. *Arkansas Gazette,* November 11 and 14, 1942; Anderson, "Early Reaction in Arkansas to the Relocation of Japanese in the State," 205; Vickers, "Japanese-American Relocation," 175; Johnston Narrative, 2; Leflar to Glick, December 4, 1942, File Box 4, Folder 29, Leflar Papers; Johnston Narrative, 2.

40. Adkins to California Secretary of State, December 3, 1943, General Correspondence, Section III, A, Folder 78, Adkins Papers.

41. *Arkansas Democrat,* January 5, 1943; *Arkansas Gazette,* January 5, 13, and February 14, 1943; *Acts of Arkansas* (Little Rock, 1943), 75.

42. "News Notes of Historical Interest," *Arkansas Historical Quarterly,* 2 (March 1943); 88; *Arkansas Gazette,* February 10, 1943; *Pine Bluff Commercial,* February 18, 1943.

43. *Arkansas Democrat,* July 4, 1943; Smith's Report, April 2, 1943; Paul A. Taylor, project director, to John H. Provinse, chief, Community Services, War Relocation Authority, July 24, 1943. War Relocation Authority, Community Analyst Section, Record Group 210, Box 17, Folder 1, National Archives. Hereafter only names, dates, and locations of materials from this collection will be cited; Bob Kuno to Virginia Tidball (no date or month given), 1943, Student Essays, Folder 1, Virginia Tidball Papers, University of Arkansas Library, Fayetteville. Ms. Tidball was an English teacher at the Jerome Relocation Center. Hereafter only names and location of correspondence will be cited.

44. Showphie Horie, "My Autobiography," Student Essays, January 17, 1943, Folder 1, Tidball Papers.

45. A. Higake, "My Autobiography," Student Essays, August 12, 1943. Folder 1, Tidball Papers.

46. George Fukumoto (McGehee), to the Editor, *Arkansas Gazette,* May 28, 1945.

47. Charles Wisdom, community analyst, Rohwer, Final Report, July, 1944, War Relocation Authority, RG 210, Box 18, Folder 6; Frank F. Arakawa, chairman, Jerome Community Council, Weekly Report to Edgar C. McVoy, social science analyst, Jerome, April 8, 1944, War Relocation Authority, Community Analyst Section, RG 210, Box 17, Folder 2, Document 140; Ray D. Johnston, project director, Rohwer Relocation Center to Dillon S. Meyer, War Relocation Authority, Resettlement Program, Box 18, Folder 2, Document 18.

48. Dorr, "Issei, Nisei, and Arkansas," 185.

49. Frank F. Arakawa, chairman, Jerome Community Council, Weekly Report to Edgar C. McVoy, social science analyst, Jerome, April 8, 1944, WRA, RG 210, Box 17, Folder 2, Document 140; Cash Cade, "Japanese-Americans Settle in Pulaski County," *Arkansas Democrat,* "Sunday Magazine," July 1, 1945, 2–3.

Chapter 5

1. *Arkansas Gazette,* March 6, 1940.

2. *Arkansas Gazette,* March 24, 1940.

3. *Arkansas Gazette,* December 6, 1940; *Northwest Arkansas Times,* October 21, 1941.

4. *Arkansas Gazette,* March 6, 1940, and May 9, 1941; *Pine Bluff Commercial,* May 19, 1941; Editorial, *Arkansas State Press,* May 16 and 23, 1941. All materials taken from this black owned and operated weekly come from editorials.

5. Michael L. Sovern, *Legal Restraints on Racial Discrimination in Employment* (New York, 1966), 9.

6. Perrett, *Days of Sadness, Years of Triumph*, 143.

7. *Atkins Chronicle*, October 16, 1942.

8. William C. Yarbrough to Homer M. Adkins, August 16, 1941, Miscellaneous Correspondence, Folder 83, Section III. Yarbrough's report identifies only the patrolman's last name, Mason. The Papers of Governor Homer M. Adkins, Arkansas History Commission, Little Rock. Hereafter only names, dates, and location will be cited for this collection; *Arkansas Gazette*, August 15 and 16, 1971.

9. *Arkansas Democrat*, March 23 and 26, 1942; *Arkansas Gazette*, March 23, 24, and 26, 1942; Daisy Bates, *The Long Shadow of Little Rock* (New York, 1962), 35; Pittsburg *Courier*, December 21, 1941.

10. Bates, *The Long Shadow of Little Rock*, 35.

11. *Arkansas Democrat*, March 30, 1942; *Arkansas Gazette*, March 30, 1942; Bates, *The Long Shadow of Little Rock*, 36.

12. *State Press*, March 27 and April 5 and 10, 1942; *Arkansas Gazette*, June 11 and 12, 1942; *State Press*, June 12, 1942.

13. Bates, *The Long Shadow of Little Rock*, 37; *Arkansas Gazette*, March 30, 1942; Obituary of L. C. Bates, *Arkansas Gazette*, August 24, 1980.

14. Editorial, *Arkansas Gazette*, June 12, 1942; *Arkansas Democrat*, "Run of the News," daily column, March 23, 1942.

15. *Arkansas Gazette*, March 30, 1942.

16. *State Press*, August 21, 1942; *Arkansas Gazette*, June 12 and August 13 and 19, 1942.

17. *State Press*, August 21, 1942; *Arkansas Democrat*, September 1, 1942; *Arkansas Gazette*, June 5 and September 1, 1942.

18. Lois B. Moreland, *White Racism and the Law* (Ohio, 1970), 10; *Arkansas Gazette*, March 21 and April 16, 1941; *Arkansas Democrat*, March 1, 1942.

19. *Arkansas Democrat*, March 1 and 13, 1942; *Arkansas Gazette*, March 1 and 13, 1942.

20. *Arkansas Gazette*, May 21, 1942.

21. *Arkansas Gazette*, September 20 and October 3, 1942; *Arkansas Democrat*, March 9 and October 3, 1942.

22. *Arkansas Democrat*, January 6, and Editorial, *Arkansas Democrat*, January 7, 1944; *Arkansas Gazette*, January 6, 1944, and June 20, 1945.

23. *Southwest American*, March 5, 1942; For a perceptive discussion of the "one party" South and the legal disfranchisement of blacks in Arkansas, see John W. Graces, "Negro Disfranchisement in Arkansas," *Arkansas Historical Quarterly*, 26 (1967); Darlene Clark Hines, *Black Victory: The Rise and Fall of the White Primary in Texas* (New York, 1979); V. O. Key, *Southern Politics in State and Nation* (New York, 1959); J. Morgan Kousser, *The Shaping of Southern Politics: Suffrage Restrictions and the Establishment of the One-Party South, 1890–1910* (New Haven, 1974); Steven F. Lawson, *Black Ballots: Voting Rights in the South, 1944–1949* (New York, 1976).

24. Hines, *Black Victory*, 72–85; Atkinson and Ferguson, *Historic Arkansas*, 178.

25. Atkinson and Ferguson, *Historic Arkansas*, 98–99; Hines, *Black Victory*, 72–85.

26. Numerous anti-poll tax letters were sent to the editors of various Arkansas newspapers. See Frank P. Pitts (England), to the Editor, *Arkansas Gazette*, February 29, 1940; John Q. Wolfe (Batesville), to the Editor, *Arkansas Gazette*, May 25, 1940; E. C. Forges (Greenwood), to the Editor, *Southwest American*, January 17, 1943; L. A. Smith (Greenwood), to the Editor, *Southwest American*, November 28, 1943; Editorial, *Arkansas Gazette*, February 15, 1940.

27. Editorial, *Southwest American*, January 6, 1943.

28. *State Press*, November 27, 1942.

29. Miss Evelyn Key, McNeil, Arkansas, to Congressman Oren Harris, November 20, 1942; Harris to Key, November 27, 1942, folder 242. The Congressional Papers of Oren Harris, 1926–1966, University of Arkansas Library, Fayetteville; *Arkansas Gazette*, May 30 and November 27, 1943.

30. *Arkansas Gazette*, June 9 and December 8, 1943.

31. *Arkansas Gazette*, February 9, 1943.

32. Blum, *V Was for Victory*, 233.

33. Blum, *V Was for Victory*, 288; Polenberg, *War and Society*, 196; Perrett, *Days of Sadness, Years of Triumph*, 288.

34. Editorial, *Southwest American*, September 11, 1943; Karr Shannon (Melbourne), to the Editor, *Arkansas Gazette*, January 27, 1944; *Arkansas Gazette*, November 22, 1943.

35. Quoted in Polenberg, *War and Society*, 197.

36. *Arkansas Gazette*, December 8, 1940, and June 7, 1942.

37. Blum, *V Was for Victory*, 1942; *State Press*, September 26, 1941, and July 17, 1942.

38. *Arkansas Gazette*, July 27 and 29, 1942; *The New York Times*, July 26 and 29, 1942; *Pine Bluff Commercial*, July 29, 1942.

39. Moreland, *White Racism and the Law*, 86; *Arkansas Democrat*, April 5, 1944; *Pine Bluff Commercial*, April 5, 1944; the best account of the event leading to the *Smith v. Allwright* decision and the ramifications of the Court's ruling is Hines, *Black Victory*.

40. *Arkansas Gazette*, April 4, 1944; *State Press*, July 21, 1944.

41. Homer M. Adkins to Joe C. Barrett, chairman, State Democratic Committee, May 18, 1944, Official Correspondence, Section III, Folder 85. The Papers of Governor Homer M. Adkins, Arkansas History Commission, Little Rock. Hereafter only names, dates, and location of correspondence will be cited.

42. *Arkansas Gazette*, April 5, 13, and June 30, 1944; *Arkansas Democrat*, April 5 and June 31, 1944.

43. *Arkansas Democrat*, May 28, 30, and June 30, 1944.

44. Adkins to Barrett, July 5, 1944, Adkins Papers, Official Correspondence, Section III, Folder 289.

45. *Arkansas Democrat*, July 25, 1944; *Arkansas Gazette*, July 26, 1944; *Northwest Arkansas Times*, July 26, 1944.

46. *Arkansas Gazette*, September 16 and 17, 1944; *The New York Times*, September 17, 1944.

47. *The New York Times*, February 20, 1945; *Arkansas Democrat*, February 23, 1945; *Arkansas Gazette*, February 20 and 24, 1945; *Benton County Democrat*, March 15, 1945; *Southwest American*, February 13, 1945.

48. *Arkansas Democrat*, February 23 and 27, 1945; *Arkansas Gazette*, February 20, 24, 27, and 28, 1945. The double-primary system established by the 1945 legislature was repealed in 1950 due to rising costs and public complaints.

49. Editorial, *Marked Tree Tribune*, November 21, 1945.

50. *Southwest American*, February 21, 1945; *State Press*, November 9, 1945; *Arkansas Democrat*, November 21, 1945; *Arkansas Gazette*, November 21, 1945.

51. Mrs. Mary B. Saladino, Washington, D.C., to J. William Fulbright, March 28, 1944, Box 48, Folder 2. The Congressional Papers of J. W. Fulbright, University of Arkansas Library, Fayetteville; Private Pat Dunnahoo, United States Army, to Senator J. William Fulbright, June 15, 1945; Fulbright to Dunnahoo, June 30, 1945, Fulbright Papers, Box 48, Folder 2.

Chapter 6

1. Perrett, *Days of Sadness, Years of Triumph*, 404; *Arkansas Gazette*, November 10, 1945.

2. Perrett, *Days of Sadness, Years of Triumph*, 406.

3. For a detailed account of the Farm Security Administration's experiment with collective farming, see James D. Holley, *The New Deal and Farm Tenancy: Rural Resettlement in Arkansas, Louisiana, and Mississippi* (Baton Rouge, 1969), and Nash, *The Great Depression and World War II*, 68–69.

4. *Atkins Chronicle*, August 25, 1941; Polenberg, *War and Society*, 85; *Jonesboro Evening Sun*, February 16, 1942.

5. Perrett, *Days of Sadness, Years of Triumph*, 406; Blum, *V Was for Victory*, 239.

6. *Arkansas Democrat*, March 2 and 12, 1942.

7. Editorial, *Arkansas Democrat*, February 17, 1947; *Arkansas Gazette*, March 2, 1943.

8. A. W. Oliver and John A. Cooper, West Memphis, Arkansas, to Congressman Ezekiel C. Gathings, May 31, 1943, Farm Security Administration (FSA) File. The Congressional Papers of E. C. Gathings, Dan B. Ellis Library, Arkansas State University, Jonesboro. This collection is available for research but has not been catalogued. It is roughly organized by subject matter. Hereafter materials from this collection will be cited by file heading, date, and location.

9. R. B. Shaw, president, Shaw Cotton Company, Marianna, Arkansas, to E. C. Gathings, March 23, 1943, FSA File; C. F. Tompkins, president, Mississippi County

Farm Bureau, Blytheville, to E. C. Gathings, May 25, 1943, FSA File; J. Mell Brooks, secretary, Blytheville Chamber of Commerce, to Gathings, April 17, 1943, FSA File; Otis S. Howe, president, Arkansas Agricultural Council, Little Rock, to Representative J. William Fulbright, April, 1934, FSA File; J. E. Anderson, president, First National Bank, Green Forrest, Arkansas, to J. William Fulbright, May 5, 1943, Fulbright Papers, Box 3, Folder 17. The Congressional Papers of J. W. Fulbright, University of Arkansas Library, Fayetteville, Arkansas. Hereafter only name, dates, and location of correspondence for the Fulbright collection will be cited.

10. *Arkansas Gazette*, April 18, 1943; Mr. and Mrs. George Brombaugh, Gentry, Arkansas, to Representative J. W. Fulbright, April 23, 1943, Fulbright Papers, Box 3, Folder 17.

11. John G. Pipkins, commissioner of Public Welfare, Little Rock, Arkansas, to E. C. Gathings, June 21, 1943, FSA File; J. William Fulbright to Vol Bennett, April 8, 1943, Fulbright Papers, Box 3, Folder 17; E. C. Gathings to C. F. Thompkins, president, Mississippi County Farm Bureau, May 26, 1943; Gathings to J. Mell Brooks, secretary, Blytheville Chamber of Commerce, April 24, 1943, FSA File.

12. *Arkansas Gazette*, April 23, 1943; *Marked Tree Tribune*, April 29, 1943; Polenberg, *War and Society*, 86; Perrett, *Days of Sadness, Years of Triumph*, 406–407; H. E. Baker (Danville), to the Editor, *Arkansas Gazette*, April 18, 1943.

13. *Arkansas Gazette*, March 22, 1944.

14. *Arkansas Gazette*, March 16, 1944.

15. *Arkansas Gazette*, April 6, 1941.

16. *Arkansas Gazette*, Editorial, June 10, 1941.

17. *State Press*, October 17, 1941.

18. Polenberg, *War and Society*, 106.

19. *Arkansas Gazette*, October 14, 1941; Philip Hicky to Congressman E. C. Gathings, December 9, 1941, Gathings Papers, Labor File.

20. From a copy of Congressman Gathings' anti-labor speech delivered in the House of Representatives on March 19, 1942, Gathings Papers, Labor File. For a condensed summary of the speech, see the *Arkansas Gazette*, March 19, 1942; *Arkansas Democrat*, March 19, 1942; R. B. Shaw to Gathings, March 23, 1942, Gathings Papers, FSA File.

21. Donald H. Grubbs, *Cry from the Cotton: The Southern Tenant Farmers Union and the New Deal* (Chapel Hill, 1971), 84–85.

22. *Arkansas Gazette*, February 2, 24, 25, and March 1, 1943.

23. *Arkansas Gazette*, February 25, 1943.

24. *Northwest Arkansas Times*, March 5, 1943; *Arkansas Gazette*, March 5 and May 18, 1943.

25. C. F. Byrns, "Off the Record," daily column, *Southwest American*, February 26, 1943; *Arkansas Gazette*, March 11, 1943.

26. *Arkansas Gazette*, February 25, 1943.

27. Ernest Borden (Knobel), to the Editor, *Arkansas Gazette*, February 14, 1943;

R. H. Cannon (Portland), to the Editor, *Arkansas Gazette*, February 25, 1943. Hereafter only the place and origin for letters to the editor will be cited when such letters were mailed from within Arkansas.

28. Polenberg, *War and Society*, 160–170; Perrett, *Days of Sadness, Years of Triumph*, 307; *Arkansas Gazette*, May 1, 1943.

29. Quoted in Perrett, *Days of Sadness, Years of Triumph*, 307.

30. *Arkansas Gazette*, May 1, 4, and June 5, 1943; Ernest Richards (Osceola), to the Editor, *Osceola Times* (Osceola, Arkansas), May 21, 1943.

31. Blum, *V Was for Victory*, 241; Polenberg, *War and Society*, 168.

32. *Arkansas Gazette*, June 29, 1943; W. M. Freeze to E. C. Gathings, June 26, 1943, Gathings Papers, Labor File.

33. F. Ray Marshall, *Labor in the South* (Cambridge, 1967), 241; Ferguson and Atkinson, *Historic Arkansas*, 312.

34. Ferguson and Atkinson, *Historic Arkansas*, 312; J. B. McPherson, American Federation of Labor (AFL) organizer for Arkansas to William T. Schulte, coordinator of Field Operations, War Production Board (WPB), February 26, 1944, War Manpower Commission, Record Group 211, Series 29, Box 194, National Archives. Hereafter only names, dates and Record Group will be cited for this material. For an informative discussion of German prisoners of war in Arkansas, see Merrill R. Pritchett and William L. Shea, "The Afrika Korps in Arkansas, 1943–1946," *Arkansas Historical Quarterly*, 37 (Spring, 1978).

35. N. I. Callowick, regional labor representative, WPB, to William F. Rafsky, assistant to the deputy vice-chairman, Office of Labor Production, February 26, 1944, RG 211, Series 29, Box 194.

36. Aubrey McCall (Little Rock), to the Editor, *Arkansas Gazette*, November 5, 1944; *Ibid.*, Editorial, Ferguson and Atkinson, *Historic Arkansas*, 312.

37. J. M. Evans (Leola), to the Editor, *Arkansas Gazette*, November 7, 1944.

38. Ferguson and Atkinson, *Historic Arkansas*, 312.

Chapter 7

1. *Arkansas Democrat*, May 7 and 8, 1945; *Arkansas Gazette*, May 7 and 8, 1945; *Jonesboro Evening Sun*, May 7, 1945.

2. *Arkansas Democrat*, August 15, 1945; *Arkansas Gazette*, August 15, 1945; *Southwest American*, August 15, 1945.

3. Ferguson and Atkinson, *Historic Arkansas*, 294–301.

4. *Arkansas Gazette*, August 1 and November 3, 1943; *Jonesboro Evening Sun*, July 26, 1943.

5. Paul V. McNutt, chairman, War Manpower Commission, Arkansas, Speech to the Little Rock Chamber of Commerce, May 28, 1945. Copy of speech located in Record Group 183, Department of Labor, Labor Market Survey Reports, United States Employment Service, Box 18, Arkansas; *Arkansas Gazette*, September 9, 1945; Ferguson and Atkinson, *Historic Arkansas*, 305–306.

6. *Arkansas Gazette*, June 12, 1943; Ferguson and Atkinson, *Historic Arkansas*, 309.

7. *Arkansas Gazette*, February 25 and March 1, 1943.

8. *Arkansas Gazette*, October 1, 1944; Ferguson and Atkinson, *Historic Arkansas*, 309.

9. "Unions Fight Ban," *Business Week*, October 21, 1944, 100; Ferguson and Atkinson, *Historic Arkansas*, 312.

10. *Jonesboro Evening Sun*, March 10, 1945; *Arkansas Gazette*, November 10 and 13, 1940, and September 30 and December 8, 1945.

11. *Southern Standard*, February 18, 1942; *Northwest Arkansas Times*, July 25, 1944; Perrett, *Days of Sadness, Years of Triumph*, 137; *Arkansas Gazette*, December 1, 1945.

12. *Arkansas Gazette*, May 30, June 15, July 13, and November 1, 1943.

13. *Arkansas Gazette*, February 6, 1940.

14. *Arkansas Gazette*, October 4, 1942, September 9 and November 10, 1945; *Southwest American*, January 8, 1944.

15. *Southwest Times Record*, February 11, 1940; Stinnett and Kennon, *All This and Tomorrow Too*, 181; *Arkansas Gazette*, May 6 and July 9, 1945.

16. *Arkansas Gazette*, February 16, 1944; *Atkins Chronicle*, October 16, 1942, and February 18, 1944; Ferguson and Atkinson, *Historic Arkansas*, 306.

17. "The Spirit of Marche," *Arkansas Democrat*, October 16, 1942; Editorial, *Pine Bluff Commercial*, June 6, 1942.

18. Editorial, *Southern Standard*, August 12, 1942; H. F. Jamison (Beebe), to the Editor, *Arkansas Gazette*, September 25, 1944; *Arkansas Gazette*, June 24 and 30, 1944.

19. Walter N. Turlock to J. William Fulbright, April 28, 1945, Box 74, Folder 16. The Congressional Papers of J. W. Fulbright, Mullins Library, University of Arkansas, Fayetteville. Hereafter only names, dates, and location of correspondence will be cited.

20. *Ibid.*, Claude Sharpe to Fulbright, April 10, 1945; Fulbright to J. G. Smith, vice-president, Arkansas Oak Flooring Company, Pine Bluff, September 24, 1945; *State Press*, February 22, 1946.

21. *Arkansas Democrat*, September 26, 1944; *Arkansas Gazette*, September 7, 1944.

22. *Southwest American*, August 17 and 22, 1944.

Bibliography

Government Documents and Publications

"Executive Order No. 9066," United States Army, Western Defense Command and Fourth Army, Final Report. *Japanese Evacuation from the West Coast,* John L. DeWitt. Washington: U.S. Government Printing Office, 1942.

Selective Service System. *Selective Service and Victory: The Fourth Report of the Director of Selective Service, 1944–1945.* Washington: U.S. Government Printing Office, 1948.

United States Congress. *An Act to Provide for the Common Defense by Increasing the Personnel of the Armed Forces of the United States and Providing for Its Training.* Publication L. 783, 76th Congress, Second Session, 1940, U.S. Statistics at Large. Washington: U.S. Government Printing Office, 1940.

United States Department of Labor. Records of the United States Employment Service, Labor Market Survey Reports, Arkansas, Record Group 183. Washington: National Archives.

United States Department of Labor. Records of the War Manpower Commission, General Records for the Farm Placement Service, Arkansas, Record Group 211. Washington: National Archives.

United States Government. Records of the War Relocation Authority, Community Analyst Section, Record Group 210. Washington: National Archives.

Manuscript Collections

Adkins, Homer A. The Papers of Governor Homer A. Adkins. Arkansas History Commission, Little Rock, Arkansas.

Ellis, Clyde T. The Congressional Papers of Clyde T. Ellis. Mullins Library, University of Arkansas, Fayetteville.

Fulbright, J. William. The Congressional Papers of J. W. Fulbright. Mullins Library, University of Arkansas, Fayetteville.

Futrell, J. M. The Papers of Governor J. M Futrell. Arkansas History Commission, Little Rock, Arkansas.

Gathings, Ezekiel C. The Congressional Papers of E. C. Gathings. Dean B. Ellis Library, Arkansas State University, Jonesboro, Arkansas.

Harris, Oren. The Congressional Papers of Oren Harris. Mullins Library, University of Arkansas, Fayetteville.

Hays, Brooks. Letters and Memorandums. Mullins Library, University of Arkansas, Fayetteville.

Johnston, Ray D. The Personal Narratives of Ray D. Johnston, project director, Rohwer, September 18, 1942, to December 31, 1945, War Relocation Authority. Microfilm copy, Arkansas History Commission, Little Rock, Arkansas.

Leflar, Robert A. The Papers of Robert A. Leflar. Mullins Library, University of Arkansas, Fayetteville.

Smith, Austin. The Reports of Austin Smith, Reports Division, Rohwer, War Relocation Authority, October 27, 1942, to December 31, 1945. Microfilm copy, Arkansas History Commission, Little Rock, Arkansas.

Tidball, Virginia. The Virginia Tidball Collection, Student Essays, Jerome Relocation Center, War Relocation Authority. Mullins Library, University of Arkansas, Fayetteville.

Newspapers

Arkansas Democrat (Little Rock), 1940–1945.
Arkansas Gazette (Little Rock), 1940–1945.
Arkansas Methodist (Arkadelphia), 1940–1945.
Arkansas State Press (Little Rock), 1940–1945.
Atkins Chronicle (Atkins), 1940–1945.
Batesville Weekly Record (Batesville), 1940–1945.
Benton County Democrat (Benton), 1940–1945.
Jonesboro Evening Sun (Jonesboro), 1940–1945.
Marked Tree Tribune (Marked Tree), 1940–1945.
Marshall Mountain Wave (Searcy), 1940–1945.
The McGehee Times (Arkansas), 1940–1945.
The New York Times (New York), 1940–1945.
Northwest Arkansas Times (formerly the *Fayetteville Daily Democrat*), 1940–1945.
Pine Bluff Commercial (Pine Bluff), 1940–1945.
Pittsburgh Courier (Pittsburgh, Penn.), 1940–1945.
Sharp County Record (Batesville), 1940–1945.
Southern Standard (Arkadelphia), 1940–1945.
Southwest American (Fort Smith), 1940–1945.

Periodicals

Anderson, William C. "Early Reaction in Arkansas to the Relocation of Japanese in the State," *Arkansas Historical Quarterly*, 23 (Autumn 1964): 195–211.

Beaker, J. A., and J. G. McNeeley. "Land Tenure in Arkansas, The Farm Tenancy Situation," *Arkansas Agricultural Experiment Station Bulletin No. 384.* (January 1940).

Cobb, William H., and Donald H. Grubbs. "Arkansas' Commonwealth College and the Southern Tenant Farmers Union," *Arkansas Historical Quarterly,* 25 (Winter 1966): 293–311.

Graves, John W. "Negro Disfranchisement in Arkansas," *Arkansas Historical Quarterly,* 26 (Autumn 1967): 199–225.

Lisenby, Foy. "A Survey of Arkansas' Image Problem," *Arkansas Historical Quarterly,* 30 (Spring 1971): 60–71.

Mitchell, H. L. "The Founding and Early History of the Southern Tenant Farmers Union," *Arkansas Historical Quarterly,* 32 (Winter 1973): 342–369.

Robinson, Mary. "Women Workers in Two Wars," *Monthly Labor Review,* 57 (October 1943): 650–671.

Rosencrantz, Florence L. "The Rice Industry in Arkansas," *Arkansas Historical Quarterly,* 5 (Summer 1946): 123–137.

Vickers, Ruth P. "Japanese-American Relocation," *Arkansas Historical Quarterly,* 10 (Summer 1951): 168–176.

Books

Blum, John Morton. *V Was for Victory: Politics and American Culture during World War II.* New York, 1976.

Conrad, David Eugene. *The Forgotten Farmers, The Story of Sharecroppers in the New Deal.* Urbana, 1965.

DuVall, Leland, ed. *Arkansas Colony and State.* Little Rock, 1973.

Ferguson, John L., and J. H. Atkinson, *Historic Arkansas.* Little Rock, 1966.

Franklin, John Hope. *From Slavery to Freedom: A History of Negro Americans.* New York, 1967.

Grodzins, Merton. *Americans Betrayed: Politics and the Japanese Evacuation.* Chicago, 1949.

Grubbs, Donald H. *Cry from the Cotton: The Southern Tenant Farmers Union and the New Deal.* Chapel Hill, 1971.

Hays, Brooks. *A Southern Moderate Speaks.* Chapel Hill, 1959.

Heard, Alexander, and Donald S. Strong. *Southern Primaries and Elections, 1920–1949.* Alabama, 1950.

Higgins, Earl Leroy. *Source Readings in Arkansas History.* Little Rock, 1964.

Hines, Darlene Clark. *Black Victory: The Rise and Fall of the White Primary in Texas.* New York, 1979.

Holley, James D. *The New Deal and Farm Tenancy: Rural Resettlement in Arkansas, Louisiana, and Mississippi.* Baton Rouge, 1969.

Jehovah's Witnesses and the War. American Civil Liberties Union. New York, 1943.

Key, V. O. *Southern Politics in State and Nation.* New York, 1959.

Kirkendall, Richard S. *The United States, 1929–1945: Years of Crisis and Change.* St. Louis, 1974.

Kitano, Harry H. L. *Japanese-Americans: The Evolution of a Subculture.* New Jersey, 1969.

Kousser, Morgan J. *The Shaping of Southern Politics: Suffrage Restrictions and the Establishment of the One-Party South, 1890–1910.* New Haven, 1974.

Langer, William L., and Everett S. Gleason. *The Undeclared War, 1940–1941.* New York, 1953.

Lawson, F. Steven. *Black Ballots: Voting Rights in the South, 1944–1949.* New York, 1976.

Leuchtenberg, William E. *Franklin D. Roosevelt and the New Deal.* New York, 1963.

Meyer, Dillon S. *Uprooted Americans.* Tucson, 1971.

Moreland, Lois B. *White Racism and the Law.* Ohio, 1970.

Morris, Richard B., et al. *America: A History of the People.* Chicago, 1971.

Nash, Gerald D. *The Great Depression and World War II: Organizing America, 1933–1945.* New York, 1979.

Patterson, James T. *The New Deal and the States.* Princeton, 1969.

Perrett, Geoffrey. *Days of Sadness, Years of Triumph: The American People, 1939–1945.*

Polenberg, Richard. *War and Society: The United States, 1941–1945.* New York, 1972.

Public Education in Arkansas: A Survey. Little Rock: Arkansas Public Expenditure Council, 1945.

Schlesinger, Arthur M. *The Coming of the New Deal.* Boston, 1959.

———. *The Politics of Upheaval, Vol. 3, The Age of Roosevelt.* Boston, 1960.

Shannon, David E. *20th Century America, World War II and Since.* Vol. 3. Chicago, 1974.

Sibley, Mulford Q., and Philip E. Jacob. *Conscription of Conscience: The American State and the Conscientious Objector, 1940–1947.* New York, 1952.

Simkins, Francis Butler, and Charles P. Roland. *A History of the South.* New York, 1972.

Stinnett, T. M., and Clara B. Kennon. *All This and Tomorrow Too: The Evolution and Continuing History of the Arkansas Education Association.* Little Rock, 1969.

Tindall, George Brown. *The Emergence of the New South, 1913–1945.* Baton Rouge, 1967.

Vernon, Walter N. *Methodism in Arkansas, 1816–1976.* Little Rock, 1976.

Williams, Harry Lee. *Forty Years behind the Scenes in Arkansas Politics.* Little Rock, 1949.

Wolters, Raymond. *Negroes and the Great Depression: The Problem of Economic Recovery.* Westport, Conn., 1970.

Unpublished Materials

Adams, Travis Martin. "The Arkansas Congressional Delegation during the New Deal." Unpublished Master's Thesis, Vanderbilt University, 1962.

Conrad, Sidney R. "The Poll Tax." Unpublished Master's Thesis, University of Arkansas, Fayetteville, 1944.

Dorr, Guy E. "Issei, Nisei, and Arkansas: A Geographic Study of the Wartime Relocation on Japanese-Americans in Southeast Arkansas." Unpublished Master's Thesis, University of Arkansas, Fayetteville, 1977.

Drummond, Boyce Alexander. "Arkansas Politics: A Study of a One-Party System." Unpublished Ph.D. Dissertation, University of Chicago, 1957.

Griner, James Emmett Pool. "The Growth of Manufacturing in Arkansas, 1900–1950." Unpublished Ph.D. Dissertation, George Peabody College for Teachers, 1958.

Rison, David E. "Arkansas during the Great Depression." Ph.D. Dissertation, University of California, Los Angeles, 1974.

Sharp, Floyd. "Traveling Recovery Road: The Story of Work Relief in Arkansas, August 1932 to November 1936." Little Rock, Arkansas History Commission, 1936.

Personal Interviews

Harrison, Henry. Rice mill superintendent during World War II, Harrisburg, Arkansas (Retired). Current Residence, Jonesboro, Arkansas. Interviewed on June 13, 1977.

Lillian, Hazel Peterson. Catering Service, University of Arkansas, 1941–1946. Current position, employee, Student Union, University of Arkansas, Fayetteville. Interviewed on July 7, 1977.

Matthews, Marshall. Research chemist, Pine Bluff Arsenal, Pine Bluff, Arkansas, 1942–1946. Current position, professor of mathematics, Arkansas State University, Jonesboro, Arkansas. Interviewed on September 14, 1977.

Thiede, Dale. Jehovah's Witness and Conscientious Objector, World War II, Little Rock, Arkansas. Interviewed on November 10, 1983. This person was also the source for copies of the correspondence between Albert H. Blakely (Conscientious Objector and Witness, World War II) and General Lewis B. Hershey, national director of Selective Service, June, 1943.

Index